THE ARCHIES

Scotland's 1000 metre mountains

...and the story of our epic journey over all 130 of them

Paul Fettes with Nicky Conway with our baton 'Rabbie' on top of Ben Nevis. Photo: Paul Fettes

Text by Paul Fettes & Friends for The Archie Foundation.

Design and layout by Tide Graphic Design Consultants Ltd.

Set in 10pt Museo Sans.

Printed by Bell & Bain, Glasgow.

ISBN- 978-1-5272-1133-9

Contact details, accommodation and travel information are correct at the time of going to press.

While every effort has been made to contact copyright holders, we apologise for any who have been inadvertently overlooked.

The maps in this book are intended as a rough guide and should not be used for navigational purposes in the field.

All the costs of graphic design and printing have been covered with substantial sponsorship by Medical + Dental Financial Planning Services, and by a very generous donation by a member of the ARCHIE Foundation Tayside Fundraising committee. The writing, editing and proofreading was a labour if love and was done for free. Therefore all the money paid for the book will go to ARCHIE apart from any sales cost (if you have bought this in a shop) and delivery cost.

FRONT COVER
Main photo: Colin Donald on the North Glen Shiel Ridge. Photo: Andrew Forrester
Left to right: Andrew Forrester and Colin Donald on North Glen Shiel Ridge. Photo: Colin Donald, Steve Manning on Bynack More. Photo: Paul Fettes Kayakers set off down Loch Etive. Photo: Kate Annan. Tom Fardon sets off from Loch Treig towards Creag Meagaidh. Photo: Alan Carson Kate Annan and Kate Boocock on Meall Ghaordaidh. Photo: Kate Annan

BACK COVER
Main photo: Ben Nevis looming behind Carn Mor Dearg, from Aonach Beag. Photo: Jason Hardy
Left to right: Russell Duncan on Sgor an Lochain Uaine (Angel's Peak) in the Cairngorms. Photo: Jason Hardy, Graeme Gatherer on Loch Etive with the Black Mount, Glencoe in the background. Photo: David Henderson, Jason Hardy and Russell Duncan on Sgurr Choinnach Mor, Grey Corries. Photo: Russell Duncan

THE ARCHIES

Scotland's 1000 metre mountains

...and the story of our epic journey over all 130 of them

THE ARCHIE FOUNDATION

MAKING THE DIFFERENCE
IN THE TAYSIDE CHILDREN'S HOSPITAL

```
0      100     200     300     400     500     600     700     800     900    1000
```

Paul Fettes & Friends

Foreword by Mark Beaumont

To my parents, Peter and Mary for leading the way,
To Heidi for supporting me on the journey,

And to Ben, Magnus and Anna for what is yet to come. I hope you
find some sort of inspiration in this book, whatever path you choose.

And to all my friends old and new who have contributed to
the Challenge, or to writing this book.

Paul.

Ben Nevis **1345m** Ben Macdui **1309m** Braeriach **1296m** Cairn Toul **1291m** Sgor an Lochain Uaine **1258m** Cairn Gorm **1244m** Aonach Beag **1234m** Aonach Mor **1221m** Carn Mor Dearg **1220m** Ben Lawers **1214m** Beinn a'Bhuird **1197m** Carn Eige (Carn Eighe) **1183m** Beinn Mheadhoin **1182m** Mam Sodhail **1181m** Stob Choire Claurigh **1177m** Ben More **1174m** Ben Avon **1171m** Stob Binnein **1165m** Beinn Bhrotain **1157m** Derry Cairngorm **1155m** Lochnagar **1155m** Sgurr nan Ceathreamhnan **1151m** Sgurr na Lapaich **1150m** Bidean nam Bian **1150m** Ben Alder **1148m** Geal-charn **1132m** Binnein Mor **1130m** Ben Lui **1130m** An Riabhachan **1129m** Creag Meagaidh **1128m** Ben Cruachan **1126m** Carn nan Gabhar **1121m** A'Chralaig **1120m** Sgor Gaoith **1118m** An Stuc **1118m** Meall Garbh **1118m** Stob Coire Easain **1115m** Stob Coire nan Lochan **1115m** Monadh Mor **1113m** Tom a'Choinich **1112m** Sgurr Mor **1110m** Sgurr nan Conbhairean **1109m** Meall a'Bhuiridh **1108m** Stob a'Choire Mheadhoin **1105m** Beinn Ghlas **1103m** Mullach Fraoch-choire **1102m** Beinn Eibhinn **1102m** Creise **1100m** Sgurr a'Mhaim **1099m** Sgurr Choinnich Mor **1094m** Sgurr nan Clach Geala **1093m** Bynack More **1090m** Stob Ghabhar **1090m** Beinn a'Chlachair **1087m** Beinn Dearg **1084m** Sgurr a'Choire Ghlais **1083m** Schiehallion **1083m** Beinn a'Chaorainn **1082m** Beinn a'Chreachain **1081m** Ben Starav **1078m** Beinn Sheasgarnich **1078m** Beinn Dorain **1076m** Stob Coire Sgreamhach **1072m** Braigh Coire Chruinn-bhalgain **1070m** An Socach **1069m** Meall Corranaich **1069m** Glas Maol **1068m** Sgurr Fhuaran **1067m** Cairn of Claise **1064m** Bidein a'Ghlas Thuill **1062m** Sgurr Fiona **1060m** Spidean a'Choire Leith **1055m** Toll Creagach **1054m** Stob Poite Coire Ardair **1054m** Sgurr a'Chaorachain **1053m** Beinn a'Chaorainn **1052m** Glas Tulaichean **1051m** Sgurr Fhuar-thuill **1049m** Geal Charn **1049m** Creag Mhor **1047m** Glas Leathad Mor **1046m** Chno Dearg **1046m** Cruach Ardrain **1046m** Beinn Iutharn Mhor **1045m** Stob Coir'an Albannaich **1044m** Meall nan Tarmachan **1044m** Carn Mairg **1041m** Sgurr na Ciche **1040m** Meall Ghaordie **1039m** Beinn Achaladair **1038m** Carn a'Mhaim **1037m** Sgurr na Lapaich **1036m** Sgurr a'Bhealaich Dheirg **1036m** Gleouraich **1035m** Carn Dearg **1034m** Beinn Fhada **1032m** Am Bodach **1032m** Carn an Righ **1029m** Carn Gorm **1029m** Ben Oss **1029m** Sgurr a'Mhaoraich **1027m** Sgurr na Ciste Duibhe **1027m** Ben Challum **1025m** Sgorr Dhearg **1024m** Mullach an Rathain **1023m** Stob Dearg **1022m** Aonach air Chrith **1021m** Ladhar Bheinn **1020m** Mullach Coire Mhic Fhearchair **1019m** Beinn Bheoil **1019m** Mullach Clach a'Bhlair **1019m** Garbh Chioch Mhor **1013m** Beinn Udlamain **1011m** Stob na Doire **1011m** Beinn Ime **1011m** Ruadh-stac Mor **1010m** Sgurr an Doire Leathain **1010m** The Saddle **1010m** Sgurr Eilde Mor **1010m** Beinn Dearg **1008m** Maoile Lunndaidh **1007m** An Sgarsoch **1006m** Beinn Fhionnlaidh **1005m** Sgurr an Lochain **1004m** Beinn an Dothaidh **1004m** Sgurr Mor **1003m** Sgurr na Carnach **1002m** Aonach Meadhoin **1001m** Sgorr Dhonuill **1001m** Meall Greigh **1001m** www.archiesmountainchallenge.org.uk

THE ARCHIES   Scotland's 1000 metre mountains

Contents

Foreword by Mark Beaumont   8

Introduction by Paul Fettes   11

Reaching 1km into the sky   14

Planning a 'bonkers and wonderful' challenge   18

Day 1	6 Archies	North Sea toe dip and northerly peaks	32
Day 2	4 Archies	Great Wilderness and Torridon	42
Day 3	5 Archies	Strathcarron to Loch Mullardoch	50
Day 4	5 Archies	Mullardoch to Affric via the Carn Eighe horseshoe	62
Day 5	7 Archies	Glen Affric to Glen Shiel	70
Day 6	7 Archies	Kintail	82
Day 7	6 Archies	Glen Shiel to Loch Quoich via Knoydart	92
Day 8	3 Archies	Loch Quoich to Loch Arkaig	106
Day 9	6 Archies	Loch Arkaig to Glen Feshie	118
Day 10	16 Archies	Central Cairngorms	124
Day 11	10 Archies	Lochnagar to Blair Atholl	140
Day 12	12 Archies	Blair Atholl to Spean Bridge via Ben Alder group	154
Day 13	13 Archies	Spean Bridge via the Mamores and Ben Nevis to Glen Coe	164
Day 14	10 Archies	Glen Coe to Glen Lyon via Loch Etive	178
Day 15	14 Archies	Glen Lyon to Strathfillan via Lawers group	188
Day 16	6 Archies	Strathfillan to Arrochar and an Atlantic toe dip	196

Winding up. Aftermath by Paul Fettes   205

Why go ARCHIE Bagging? by Russell Duncan   206

Recommended reading   210

The ARCHIE Foundation by Kevin McCormick   214

Acknowledgements   220

Foreword
By Mark Beaumont

'What a great idea! Why has this not been done before?'

When Paul first explained the concept of the Archies, the 1000 metre mountains of Scotland, I immediately loved it. Ideas that have the ability to capture the imagination and go viral are always ones that simplify the complex, and reimagine the familiar. We love our mountains in Scotland, but we climb in feet, yet navigate in metres – a rather odd situation if you stop and think about it.

My own connection to the Scottish mountains came from growing up in rural Perthshire, where Glenshee was closer than high school. Being home schooled during primary years meant a life in the great outdoors. In fact my next-door neighbour was the head of ski patrol, and so on snowy days I would often get a lift north, instead of the bus south!

Over recent years I have been proud to support the work of the Archie Foundation, especially since becoming a father myself and understanding their incredible work. I have been so impressed with the dedicated community of fundraisers, including Dr Paul Fettes and friends.

The Archie Mountain Challenge gives us a way of seeing Scotland in a new and exciting way. Landscapes that we take for granted, can be re-explored and appreciated. A relay over the 130 highest mountains in Scotland, carrying the Archie mascot, a cuddly wee rabbit, on foot, by bike and by kayak.

People are so used to flying or driving between places, which means we are removed from any real connection to the landscapes and cultures. But human powered journeys open all of our senses and allow us to truly appreciate the world we live in.

The concept of the 1000m mountains is a brilliant one. Since all the maps have been metric for decades, it makes sense to have a list of mountains in metres. This challenge and this book also introduces the concept of Archie 'bagging', as a more achievable, and dare-I-say more relevant target than the Munros. And if it were needed, here is another great reason to explore the beauty of the Scottish outdoors.

Mark Beaumont

Paul and I met up several times before the Archie Mountain Challenge to help with publicity and fundraising. I had really hoped to join in, to climb a few Archies, but unfortunately the challenge happened in the immediate aftermath of my world record ride from Cairo to Cape Town, so I had to support from afar. But now that the challenge has been set, I look forward to going back and exploring the Scottish Archies.

I was also keen to be involved because both my daughters were born in Ninewells Hospital in Dundee and being a father has highlighted to me the importance of high quality health care.

My contact with Paul has led to me becoming a Patron of the ARCHIE Foundation. The work they do in 'making a difference' to sick children in many parts of Scotland is wonderful. The money raised by this challenge will be used to create a world class twin paediatric theatre suite and will contribute a huge amount to the care of children in Tayside.

This Archie Mountain Challenge book is a superb account of a monumental challenge. It took an enormous amount of hard work and organisation by an extraordinary team to make this happen. The photography brings to life the first hand accounts of a journey through Scotland that I expect will become a famous and well-trodden one.

Very well done to Paul and friends for their imagination, dedication and camaraderie.

Mark Beaumont

Paul by the Cromarty Firth at the start of the Challenge. Photo: Magnus Fettes

INTRODUCTION

Introduction
By Paul Fettes

'How are you feeling, Dad?'
'Oh, a bit stiff, but at least it's not rigor mortis.'

I watch the stooped and rather gaunt figure of my 74-year-old father shuffle painfully and slowly towards me with the 'festinant' gait of someone with marked Parkinson's disease. It is August 2016 and the family is in a cottage in Barisdale in the remote wilderness of Knoydart. Watching him I can scarcely credit the fact that yesterday, complete with hip and knee replacements, and despite strong winds and heavy rain, he dragged himself up to the giddy heights of Ladhar Bheinn, all 1020m of it from sea level. We took a small boat in the day before. Today we will take five hours or so to walk out with our kit, in gale-force winds and lashing rain along a rough, boggy, undulating six-mile track back to Kinloch Hourn and the road home. It is just over a year since the completion of the ARCHIE Mountain Challenge, which linked all the 130 mountains in Scotland over 1000m high. It has been the inspiration for my father's heroic effort, and the weather does not dampen our spirits. This was his 129th such peak. One to go – Mullach Coire Mhic Fhearchair – in the middle of the Great Wilderness. If only he hadn't left the really remote ones till the end!

I think back just over a year to 5th June 2015, and Day 7 of the Archie Challenge. That day our intrepid team summited six 1000m mountains including Ladhar Bheinn, travelling between these remote and isolated peaks by human power alone. Starting at the campsite at Shiel Bridge, a short road cycle was followed by a run over the three 'Archies' of the South Shiel Ridge, then a cyclo-cross ride to Kinloch Hourn and a run into Barisdale and over Ladhar Bheinn. Rabbie, our cuddly rabbit baton, was then ferried back to Kinloch Hourn by sea kayak, before more cycling preceded runs up the two peaks north of Loch Quoich – the delightfully named Sgurr a'Mhaoraich ('peak of the shellfish') and Gleouraich ('peak of wild animals'). These feats seem almost inconceivable now, but this was just one day in a challenge that extended over two weeks, and the other days were just as remarkable. In total we covered over 1,700km (the distance from Edinburgh to Madrid), mainly on foot over rough terrain, and completed over 85,000m of ascent (roughly 10 times the height of Everest). What also seems hard to believe in retrospect is that our relay ran like clockwork, with no major hitches despite extreme weather conditions, and a very diverse collection of participants in a team that we endeavoured to make as inclusive as possible.

The idea for the challenge came to me on my wedding anniversary, 27 June 2014. My wife Heidi and I were walking up Ben Starav, and while I perhaps should have been paying the good lady some attention, I was thinking about a crazy challenge instead. The ARCHIE Foundation was due to be launched in Tayside later that year, and some of my more active colleagues had discussed various options for a fundraising activity that could publicise ARCHIE and raise a bit of money for the charity. Among other things, we had discussed a Land's End to John O' Groats cycle. That was a good idea, but it wasn't amazing or original, and I wanted to do something with 'wow factor'.

For some time I had been mulling over why we still think of mountains in terms of feet when all the maps have been in metres since I was a kid. Surely it is time to move into the 21st century and have a metric list of mountains. Looking down on Loch Etive in the dappled sunlight the concept for the challenge came to me in a flash – a relay over all the 1000m mountains in Scotland. By the time we got back down to the glen, I had a fairly clear idea of what the challenge would entail and had shared my ideas at length with my long-suffering better half. A relay from one end of the mountains to the other, running over the mountains, cycling and perhaps in places kayaking in between, entirely human powered with no engines involved other than for support. What an incredible journey! The details could follow later. At the time I did not know exactly which mountains would be involved or what the route would be, but I knew that it could be an amazing challenge and one that could capture hearts and minds as well as raising money for a very worthwhile cause.

This book explains why the 1000m mountains are such a great list, and why we chose to do a 'bonkers and wonderful' relay over all of them. It also tells the story of that challenge, with some personal accounts, Facebook entries, and an array of wonderful photos. Finally, the book explains why 'bagging' all of the 1000m peaks is a great personal goal, and one which is more achievable for several reasons than its (considerably) older brother, the Munro list.

Paul's parents Mary and Peter Fettes, and his younger son Magnus at the bottom of Ben Wyvis. Photo: Peter Fettes

Reaching 1km into the sky
The rationale for 1000m peaks – By Paul Fettes

'If Munro were alive today he wouldn't come up with the Munros'

From imperial to metric

Most people with any knowledge of the Scottish outdoors will have heard of the Munros. This list was created in 1891 by Sir Hugh Munro, and includes the 282 separate mountains in Scotland over 3000 feet high. Over the years this list has done wonders for hill walking and tourism in Scotland by inspiring people to climb or 'bag' each of these summits, in an activity which has become known as 'Munro bagging'. However, if Munro were alive today he wouldn't come up with a list of mountains over 3000 feet. What would be the point? There are no feet on the maps. Metrification of Ordinance Survey maps started in the 1960s and the contours and spot heights are now all in metres. In fact, the metric equivalent of 3000 feet, 914m (or 914.4m to be precise) doesn't even feature as a contour line on modern maps. Imperial measurements are irrelevant to 21st century mapping.

From opinion to clear criteria

It may surprise you to know that there are no criteria to define what makes a mountain separate from others on the list of Munros. There is no minimum height drop or minimum distance between tops. Thus what makes a mountain a Munro or merely a subsidiary 'Top' is purely down to opinion rather than any measurable separation from the peaks around it! While this may seem remarkable, it was unavoidable when Munro came up with his list in 1891. With the relatively primitive surveying techniques available at the time it is amazing that the summit heights were so well estimated. Accurate measurement of the minimum drop between two summits was not possible at the time. More than a century later this is no longer the case. With the advent of modern surveying techniques and the satellite-based Global Positioning System (GPS), it is now relatively easy to establish the 'prominence' of a mountain, with prominence being the minimum height drop between a mountain and an adjacent summit (or summits).

Joe Symonds with Rabbie on Geal Charn. Photo: Graeme Gatherer

Prominence and the list

There is a clear case for using some sort of criteria for deciding what defines a separate mountain, since we now have that technology available to us. So what should the definition be? Well, distance between peaks is not really a good way of separating two summits, which would be clear if you were on any large mountain plateau. Quite simply, what separates mountains is a difference in height. The height drop between a mountain and its surroundings (the prominence) is the best way to measure this. Prominence is now used worldwide to define lists of mountains. Because of this the Munros are arguably an outmoded concept when it comes to lists of mountains.

A good friend of mine, Nick Leslie, and I met one evening to discuss the best criteria for distinguishing separate Scottish mountains. After much deliberation (and I mean several hours poring over maps, getting rather googly eyed) we agreed that 100m is the best prominence measurement to use. This equates to a 10% drop and feels right when you look at the maps and know the mountains. Establishing the prominence of the Scottish mountains over 1000m would be a big headache and a massive logistical exercise. Fortunately, using an Internet search, we found that other people had already done the hard work, and we were able to use their list (with permission). We would therefore like to acknowledge the following people for establishing and compiling the data on the prominence of the hills: Alan Dawson, Eric Yeaman, Tony Payne, Clem Clements, Rob Woodall, Mark Jackson and Mark Trengrove.

We now had a list of 130 Scottish mountains over 1000m with 100m prominence. Interestingly, although we found that this closely matches the list of Munros over 1000m, there are some differences. Nine Munros do not make it onto the list because they do not have adequate prominence (in one case only 55m). Conversely three mountains that are over 1000m and with over 100m prominence are only listed as Munro Tops. There is no good reason why. They are all great mountains – Stob Coire nan Lochan and Stob na Doire in Glencoe, and Sgurr na Lapaich in Glen Affric (a quick search on this mountain found a hillwalking blog which states incredulously, 'This is not a Munro!!').

THE ARCHIES

Because this great list of Scottish mountains over 1000m, with 100m prominence, didn't really have a name we would like to lay claim to the name 'Archies', after The ARCHIE Foundation. We felt if we ran over all of them then we would have some justification for that claim. We also think it has a nice ring about it...

Ready for the Challenge. Some of the team in Ninewells Hospital. Photo: The Courier

Planning a 'bonkers and wonderful' challenge

By Paul Fettes

An event like this is remarkably complex and it took a year to plan. After taking a while to work out which mountains to include, we needed to plan a route. What is the optimal way to travel over 130 widely scattered mountains? Good question! How do you recruit and organise a team who can navigate over rough terrain without getting lost, injured, or worse? How do you ensure that a fresh pair of well-matched runners is available at every handover when you don't know how long each leg will take? How do you support the participants so that they are fed and rested in between legs? How do you publicise the event and ensure that it raises lots of money? These questions and many more gradually threatened to become all-consuming, so it was great that an organising committee could help spread the load.

We aimed to complete the Challenge in June 2015. The attraction of June was long daylight hours, good weather, minimal midgiedom, and it gave time for the snow to melt (or so we thought!). This gave us a year to recruit a team of willing victims and plan the Challenge.

Save the date – getting a team together

The first job was to inform as many potential participants as possible. This involved many phone calls, corridor conversations, and a big 'blanket' email to friends and acquaintances – adventure racers, mountain runners, cyclists and triathletes. It was important to give people adequate notice for involvement in the Challenge. Some might be involved for a day or two, others for a week or more. It was important to get the concept across to people, and many people were a little suspicious or even dismissive at first; but we found the more that they understood the nature of the Challenge, the more they were willing to commit to it. Notice is important for time off work and away from family or other commitments, which in many cases would lead to an overdraft of brownie points. We tried to be as inclusive as possible (which was a much greater priority than speed), but safety was clearly an issue and potential participants had to be vetted for 'mountain craft'.

Team members would also be required to perform less athletic roles. We needed people to help plan and coordinate the Challenge, and ensure a supply of runners to handover points throughout. We would also need the support of drivers, cooks, and the like. Back home, in the run up to the Challenge as well as during and after it, we would need IT support, and assistance with publicity and fundraising.

The first organisational meeting was held on 24 September 2014, and was attended by 28 people. The concept of the challenge was introduced, and many of the issues were discussed.

The first planning meeting, in Ninewells Hospital. Photo: Ben Ulyatt

Rest and Be Thankful - Planning the route

Once we had established a list of mountains, we needed to plan a route. After plotting the mountains on a map, it was clear the route could go a number of ways, but should either start at the north end or the south end. Theoretically starting at the south end meant that we would tend to have the prevailing wind helping us as we headed north-east. However, the attraction of finishing at the south end was twofold. First, the mountains were more accessible if we ran over our estimated time for completion of the Challenge and had to recruit more people at short notice. Second, and much more importantly, it meant we would finish at the pass on the A83 by Arrochar which delights in the name 'Rest and Be Thankful'. Given the heroic physical endeavours that would be required to get us to this point, this was probably the most aptly named place on the planet. Enough said!

Even planning the rough flow of a route over 130 mountains involved several of us poring over maps for hours. We tried to establish the shortest route, but also took into consideration several other factors. These included avoiding busy roads where possible for the road cycling sections, the effect of prevailing winds on long high sections such as the Nevis Range and the Cairngorm Plateau, and practicalities of handover locations.

The route was then divided into sections to be 'micro-planned' by seven individuals with experience of navigation and route planning. They were tasked with working out the optimal route for each section and the best handover points. The optimal routes had to take into account safety issues such as river crossings (bearing in mind that rivers could be in spate). Handover points would ideally be distinctive, and also easy to access. Roadside handovers were used where possible although this was not always the case, and remote handovers needed careful planning and coordination. The entire planned route was then converted into a digital map. An Excel spreadsheet was also compiled with details of each planned leg, distance and estimated time. As I am sure you can imagine, this did not happen overnight and was a bit of a labour of love. Having said that a love of the outdoors can produce a strange type of obsession, which allows the mind to run riot over a map on a dark winter's night when the real thing is a little less attractive or practical.

HarperCollins agreed to create a map of the Archies which we used as part of the subsequent press launch. They very kindly did this for free, and the map was excellent. We provided them with an Excel database of the mountains including heights and coordinates, and they marked all the summits on the map for us. The map also included a list of the mountains at the side in descending order of height.

Coast to Coast

I was very keen that the Challenge should start and finish at sea level. There was a nice symmetry about crossing the country from one end to another, and from one coast to another. It also meant that we could not be criticised for starting or finishing half way up a mountain. We would commence at the north-east end by Dingwall on the Cromarty Firth, with a toe dip in the North Sea, before cycling to the foot of our first mountain, Ben Wyvis. Our last mountain would be Ben Ime at the south-west end. While we planned a wee celebration at the Rest and Be Thankful, this would be followed by a short cycle down to the side of Loch Long by Arrochar for a toe dip in the Atlantic Ocean. I imagined warm sunshine, and a glorious victory parade, sipping champagne Tour de France style. However, the reality was that it could be a Tuesday night in the lashing rain, with the exhausted remnants of our team just keen to get it over with and get to their beds.

How long will it take? How long is a piece of string?

Estimating how long we could take to travel over 130 mountains and from one coast to another was a challenge in itself. This was important for planning purposes so that we knew what period of time to recruit people for, but also to try to ensure that the event ran smoothly. Ensuring that a fresh pair of well-matched runners was available at every handover was complicated by the fact that we had no idea how long each leg would take, let alone the whole Challenge.

We planned the event to function as a relay, but not a continuous relay, in that running over mountains in the dark might be feasible for experienced athletes in good weather, but not if it was stormy. We recognised that there would be breaks overnight, and perhaps sometimes during the day if we were short of runners, or if the weather was particularly harsh. In this respect, safety and common sense were definitely a priority over speed. We estimated that runners would average five kilometres per hour on the mountain sections (given the terrain and ascent), and that we would average 20-hour days. We estimated that road cycle legs would average 25 kph.

Paul being interviewed at the start. Photo: Magnus Fettes

Claire Hardy and John Irving on Ben Wyvis. Photo: Kirsty Duncan

Ben Ulyatt and Russell Duncan on Sgurr Fiona (An Teallach). Photo: Russell Duncan

PLANNING A BONKERS AND WONDERFUL CHALLENGE

Using this estimate we calculated that our most optimistic time for completion of the event was two weeks, but given the potential for delays due to bad weather, missed handovers etc. there was the potential for us to take a lot longer.

A spreadsheet (yes, yet another spreadsheet!) was created, which listed all the participants with contact details, capabilities (including, running, cycling, navigation etc.) and their availability. Participants for the first few days could therefore be informed which legs they would be doing, although this would need to be subject to change. Further down the Challenge, it would be more like a magical mystery tour. The key principle was to be available, and to be as flexible as possible about time and location. The Challenge was planned for the first two weeks of June 2015, but there was an understanding that it could drag on into the latter half of the month, or perhaps even into July. Only time would tell.

A cuddly baton

Any self-respecting relay worth its salt has to have a baton. Clearly lugging a great, hefty flaming torch (like the one used in the Olympic relay) over mountains in wind and rain wasn't practical, and we also wanted something that would be appropriate to a challenge in aid of a children's charity. By chance the ARCHIE Foundation already had a cuddly toy – Archie's rabbit – which appears in the ARCHIE logo. Perfect! Archie's rabbit, or 'Rabbie' as he came to be known, could be included in 'selfies' on every summit of the Challenge as part of a photographic record of where we had been. We also put a waterproof satellite tracker in a wee rucksack on Rabbie's back. This Spot Tracker was kindly provided by Mapyx for the duration of the Challenge, and would enable people to follow our every move from the comfort of their own home. It was also an important safety feature, which should enable rapid location of the baton carriers in the event of any mishap, as long as we made sure the battery did not run out.

Safety

You would not have to be a genius to realise that a challenge involving running over mountains at all hours and in all weathers has inherent risk. As well as the implied consent of signing up, we had an online registration form, which included a disclaimer. One of our team even wrote risk assessments and detailed protocols for what to do if things went wrong.

Dundonnell Mountain Rescue kindly attended the first weekend (although they were not needed!). Photo: Peter Fettes

For safety reasons we made it a rule to travel in pairs on the mountains, and in addition to the tracker, runners were required to take appropriate kit from a list that we had compiled. This was similar to the kit list for many mountain challenges and included map, compass, whistle, full body cover and warm clothing, hat, gloves, adequate supplies of food and a head torch. In addition to this we supplied runners with a first aid kit, and a 'Blizzard Pack' which is a compact, lightweight foil sleeping bag, which is vastly superior to the heavy, orange plastic survival bag that many people carry instead. The list did not include crampons or ice axe, but in the event these were taken for some of the legs. We ensured that at least one of the pair was an experienced navigator, and tried to ensure that the less experienced runners were always paired with 'old hands'.

Given that for much of the Challenge we would have limited or no mobile phone signal, we decided to hire a satellite phone for the duration. This would mean if all else failed that we should still have contact with the outside world.

Publicity, celebrities and fundraising

Publicising the event was important in order to maximise fundraising, and in order to help raise the profile of the ARCHIE Foundation, and the Tayside appeal. Newspaper coverage was easy. ARCHIE already had a very good working relationship with DC Thomson in Aberdeen, and the Dundee *Courier* had already agreed to champion and support the charity in the Tayside area. We met with an editorial group from *The Courier* and they could not have been more helpful. They agreed to cover the Challenge on an almost daily basis. There would also be a launch piece including a big fold out version of the HarperCollins map with our intended route shown, and the list of all 130 mountains (shown on page 207).

Involving celebrities seemed like an obvious way of helping to promote the Challenge. Scottish celebrities with an outdoor bent were the most obvious choices. Through local contacts Andrew Murray (the endurance running doctor, not the tennis player) was contacted and was keen to participate if he could. Chris Hoy had a new baby and politely declined to be involved in the initial cycle. However Mark Beaumont thought the Challenge was a great idea, and his reaction to the enquiring email was: 'What a great idea – why has this not been done before? ' An initial meeting over a coffee was fruitful, and Mark intended to be involved if he possibly could. He was planning to cycle the length of Africa from Cairo to Capetown in the spring of 2015, with the aim of setting a new World Record. His involvement would depend on how this went. You can read about his exploits and how he fulfilled his aim in the book *Africa Solo*. Mark was clear that to maximise fundraising potential it was imperative that the Challenge should be televised.

Triple Echo Productions and STV were both contacted. Mark Beaumont was able to pull some strings and arrange a meeting with STV. There was a possibility that they might choose to cover the event as part of the STV Children's Appeal that year, with a proportion of the proceeds going to the ARCHIE Foundation.

This was an exciting prospect, because it would be our best option for high profile fundraising, but in the end STV decided not to film our Challenge, perhaps because they felt there was a high risk we would fail and it would not make a good story. Also there may have been some degree of conflict of interest in supporting a different children's charity. In contrast, Richard Else and Margaret Wicks of Triple Echo Productions were very keen to film the Challenge for *The Adventure Show* on BBC2. Triple Echo Productions have a wealth of experience with filming in remote outdoor settings, which meant they were a reliable option for covering such a challenge. They were clear from the outset that the BBC would not overtly support the fundraising aspect of the Challenge, but mainstream TV coverage certainly wouldn't be detrimental for publicity or fundraising.

One of the fundraising aspirations was to get corporate funding and sponsorship for the Challenge. Many letters were written and applications made, but there were no positive responses for large donations. However, the John Clarke Motor Group kindly agreed to provide a support vehicle – a VW Transporter – for the duration of the Challenge, which was a welcome addition to the kind offer of a loan of a motor home from Liz Fettes (my aunt), and both of these were gratefully received. Help of this kind was incredibly important to the smooth running of the Challenge, but it wouldn't directly help kids in Tayside. Finally, with the clock ticking down towards the Challenge, Medical and Dental Financial Planning Services gave us a very generous donation. More fundraising would come through sponsorship with online and cash payments, but at least we were finally up and running!

Social media, logos and T-shirts

A 21st century challenge really should have internet presence. ARCHIE kindly set up a website for us, which still exists at www.archiesmountainchallenge.org.uk and contains many of the personal accounts included in this book. This was ably populated and maintained by Chris Kennedy, an IT guru for Dundee Medical School. Chris also set up Facebook and Twitter accounts, which ensured that we had all sorts of methods of electronic communication at our disposal. David Tipping, architect for ARCHIE, was a magician with design and created logos and banners for the

ARCHIE'S MOUNTAIN CHALLENGE

website, as well as a wonderful T-shirt which was made available in both cotton and a technical fabric for outdoor pursuits, which runners could wear during the Challenge. We were delighted with the T-shirt, which had a graphic of Archie and his rabbit on Buachaille Etive Mor on the front. On the back was a map of Scotland made out of a list of all 130 Archies in descending height order.

Extreme Team Building – Community walks and the first weekend

There were three guided walks, one on each of the three weekends of the Challenge, up to the summits of Ben Wyvis, Lochnagar and Schiehallion respectively, which were organised with the intention of including more people in the Challenge, and adding to the community spirit. Ben Wyvis was the first mountain in the Challenge, and a family friendly weekend of activities was planned as part of the launch. We arranged to stay in the Garve Hotel, and planned a quiz and various other forms of entertainment for the evening. This inaugural weekend was planned by staff members at Ninewells, with the help from the ARCHIE Highland office in Inverness. The plan was to get a bunch of NHS Tayside staff members together with family and friends, to see the runners off, climb a hill, and generally have a good team-building weekend. To reserve rooms in the hotel, we had advance booking from many members of staff from Ninewells Hospital and their families. This included paediatricians, paediatric nurses (including Alison Geddes who on the first morning was to give us a rousing send-off by playing the bagpipes), anaesthetic and theatre nurses, anaesthetists, surgeons and a cardiologist.

The Schiehallion walk was organised with help from the Tayside ARCHIE Office. Both these walks functioned as stand-alone events. We discussed the possibility of staging them to coincide with the Challenge, but this was felt to be too much of a logistic nightmare and we made the pragmatic decision to keep things simple. In the event, the walkers on Schiehallion were halfway up when they met the runners coming down, and were able to cheer them and Rabbie onwards. Although it was cold and cloudy at the top, the Schiehallion walk was an enjoyable family affair.

Lochnagar is the most easterly Archie, and nearest to Aberdeen. This walk was organised by the Aberdeen office of the ARCHIE Foundation. Unfortunately the walk had to be curtailed because of severe weather conditions. This coincided with our lowest Archie day in the main Challenge, where participants battled along a ridge in inner Knoydart. The curtailment of the Lochnagar walk unfortunately meant that octogenarian Robin Kay (86) failed to make it to the summit of his favourite mountain. He headed three generations of his family on the walk, with his daughter Vanessa (Obstetrician & Gynaecologist in Tayside, 21 and a bit) and granddaughter Isla who was 14 at the time.

Head Injury

On 23rd March 2015 I was found lying unconscious on a road. I had been out for an early morning bike ride before work on a Monday morning – 35 miles round the beautiful Carse of Gowrie, by Dundee. It was a clear morning and although it was only March it was frost-free. It is not clear why I came off my bike on the corner, but I don't think I was going too fast, and I remember being in control going into the corner, which was free of traffic. Perhaps I hit a pot-hole.

The accident was unwitnessed, but going by the time of arrival of the ambulance and my presentation to the A&E of my work hospital, I don't think I was unconscious for more than five or ten minutes. An urgent CT scan of my head showed minimally displaced fractures of my cheekbone and jawbone, but my brain looked OK. I needed a bit of cleaning up and about 30 stitches to my face. My hip hurt a lot, and although the X-Ray was reported as normal at the time, I found out about six weeks later that I actually had a fracture of the greater trochanter of my femur – in other words, I had also broken my hip.

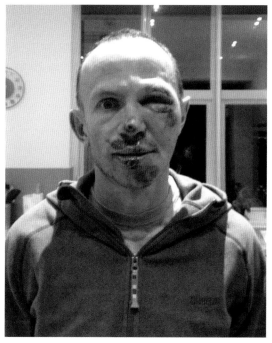

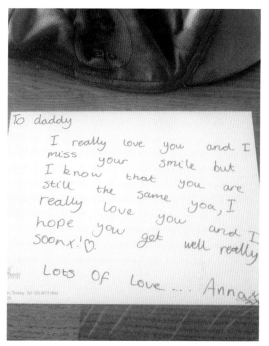

To daddy

I really love you and I miss your smile but I know that you are still the same you, I really love you, I hope you get well really soon x! ♡.

Lots of love ... Anna

Shortly after the accident. Photo: Heidi Fettes

Letter from my daughter Anna. Photo: Paul Fettes

My recollection of the ambulance ride, the short stay in the Emergency Department and the subsequent journey home is pretty patchy. I remember the shocked look on my wife and kids' faces, and how my middle son seemed to feel bad about smirking when he told me I looked like 'Sloth out of *The Goonies*'. (I hadn't seen *The Goonies*, so I Googled this and had to admit he had a point!) My main memory of the next few days is of pain, a desperate need to sleep, and feeling foggy-headed. I initially assumed that I would be fully recovered within a week. However, it soon became evident that I would take a lot longer to recover. The bones and cuts healed nicely and within a few days I looked fine, but I was still suffering from the effects of concussion, and anyone who had even a short conversation with me at this stage could tell that I was 'no right in the heid'.

It became clear that I would no longer be able to lead the organising of the Challenge. After three weeks off work, I initially struggled with a gentle phased return to work, and simply couldn't cope with anything else. We seriously considered postponing the whole thing for a year, but the date was set, much of the planning had already been done, and there was a momentum gathering. Others stepped in to plan the event, while I took a back seat and concentrated on recovering. In retrospect this was probably a good thing. I could still oversee the organisation of the Challenge in a rather devolved way, but I was freed from any hard graft. Several very capable members of the team stepped up to the mark, especially fellow anaesthetists Gillian Campbell and Ben Ulyatt, and the ARCHIE staff. If anything, my accident helped our planning to gather momentum rather than lose it.

My head injury was the biggest handicap, but my hip was still very sore. Although I didn't need surgery, it was painful to walk, and running was out of the question until about three weeks before we set off. After the accident I also had some issues with balance, and with confidence riding a bike on the roads. Ironically almost all of my training for this crazy outdoor adventure was completed on a static bike, and I had not been up a mountain for over a year! I had no idea if I would be able to participate in any meaningful way but my head started to clear about a week or so before the Challenge began, and although lacking training, I was able to take an active part in the Challenge and was not restricted by my injuries.

Raring to go

In the lead up to the Challenge, everything seemed to be fitting into place. We had some corporate sponsorship, and some online donation sites set up. We had a website and social media. We had excellent coverage in *The Courier* in the lead up to the event, plus a small feature on STV News. Some filming of the event for *The Adventure Show* was organised. We had a clear route plan, maps, a database of available athletes and support people, and an idea of who would do what for the first few days. We had support vehicles, ideas of accommodation to use, and places to camp on the way. We had arranged a bit of a family friendly shindig for the first weekend to start things off, and had three community walks organised. We had ARCHIE Foundation items for sale, including the excellent Mountain Challenge T-shirts, and we had ARCHIE gazebos and banners to use for strategic points on the route.

The Storehouse, on the Cromarty Firth, by Dingwall, had kindly agreed to host the start and to provide us with free coffee and bacon rolls. In a strange form of symmetry we had some sandwiches and a room vaguely booked in the Village Inn in Arrochar to mark the finish. Perhaps most importantly we had almost endless supplies of home baking. How could we possibly fail? Now all we needed was some good weather and things would be perfect.

A few last minute call-offs were inevitable, and required some juggling of personnel, but all the stages were covered for the first few days. The available forecasts were not great, with some precipitation and low temperatures, but as we drove north on the Friday, it was still a surprise to see a fresh dusting of icing-sugar snow on the Cairngorms from about 600m up. The Garve Hotel made an excellent base for the first weekend, in that it was very close to the base of Ben Wyvis. Forty people from our group had booked in, with almost as many again staying close by. There was an expectant air in the hotel, and surprisingly few in the bar. All was ready for an 8am start...

Rory Maguire (12) and Ben Fettes (15) at the start. Photo: Magnus Fettes

DAY 1
30 May 2015
6 ARCHIES

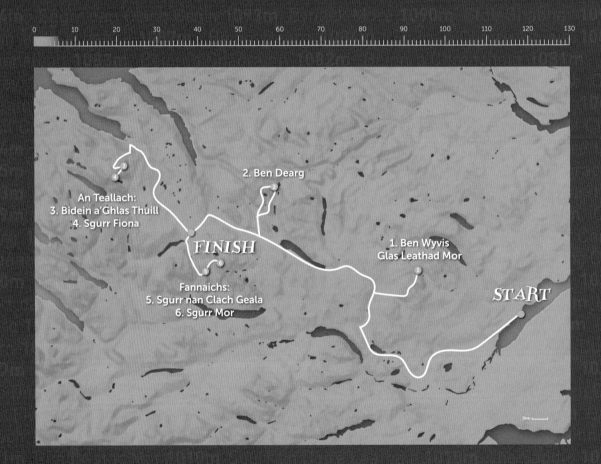

2. Ben Dearg

An Teallach:
3. Bidein a'Ghlas Thuill
4. Sgurr Fiona

FINISH

1. Ben Wyvis
Glas Leathad Mor

START

Fannaichs:
5. Sgurr nan Clach Geala
6. Sgurr Mor

START 07.53 – NORTH SEA TOE DIP

Cromarty Firth at the Storehouse, Foulis Ferry, by Dingwall:
Ben Fettes (15), Rory McGuire (12) & Paul Fettes

CYCLE – DINGWALL TO WYVIS

Ben Fettes, Rory McGuire, Chris Kennedy, Vicky Alexander, Andrew Kilpatrick, Craig
Cumming, Ben Ulyatt, Paul Fettes, Barry McGuire & Simon Crawley. 36km (480m)*

BEN WYVIS

1. Glas Leathad Mor (1046m): Claire Hardy, Kirsty Duncan & John Irving. 14km (860m)

CYCLE

Wyvis to Dearg: Barry McGuire & Rory McGuire. 22km (140m)

BEN DEARG

2: Ben Dearg (1084m): Simon Crawley & Jason Hardy. 13km (880m)

CYCLE TO DUNDONALD

Barry McGuire & Rory McGuire. 24km (330m)

AN TEALLACH

3. Bidein a'Ghlas Thuill (1062m), 4. Sgurr Fiona (1060m): Russell Duncan & Ben Ulyatt.
15km (1190m)

CYCLE TO FANNAICHS

Russell Duncan & Ben Ulyatt 16km (390m)

FANNAICHS

5. Sgurr nan Clach Geala (1093m), 6. Sgurr Mor (1110m): Grant Rodney & Nick Leslie.
21km (1080m)

*Distance in kilometres, (and ascent in metres – this is the cumulative ascent of the leg, even if there is a net descent and the finish
is lower than the start). In some cases there was a walk (or run) in or out to the start or finish of a leg without carrying the baton.

First Archie: Ben Wyvis
By John Irving – with Claire Hardy and Kirsty Duncan

I never get picked first for anything, so I didn't know what to make of it, seeing my name against leg one of the Archie Mountain Challenge, up and down Ben Wyvis. I was sure I had explained that I could do a bit of slow hill running, and had emphasised the slow. When I do a hill race I tend to stand out from the crowd, a well-nourished Labrador among the greyhounds; I don't think I have ever finished in the front half of the field. Yet there I was paired up with Claire Hardy and Kirsty Duncan to run up the first Archie in front of a jamboree of families, supporters, sponsored walkers, journalists and cameramen assembled at Garve.

I arrived late on the Friday night, and met Kirsty and Claire at the Ben Wyvis car park on the Saturday morning. Introductions were made and filmed for *The Courier*. The hills were clagged in but it was a good Scottish Summer Day – it wasn't raining much and there were no midges. Crowds of children and parents fussed into cagoules and waterproof trousers. Woolly hats covered every hairstyle from four-year-old pigtails to 70-year-old grey. A shout announced the arrival of the cyclists. There were no formalities with the handover of Rabbie the tracker rabbit. He left a cyclist's pocket, was strapped onto a rucksack, and we were off.

We zoomed off along the track, at parkrun pace. A sudden fear struck after a minute of this: 'Are we going the right way?' But we were, and pushed hard up the track through the woods. I managed to get my breath back when we stopped for waterproofs and hats as the path rose into the cloud. The pace settled into a rapid walk and the summit plateau arrived quickly. There was good running here on the shallow moss and the firm snow patches. The summit appeared on schedule, with a well wrapped-up *Adventure Show* camera operative, who requested a second arrival for the warmed-up camera. Cold batteries and cold fingers fumbled through some summit selfies, and we headed back. Down to the sponsored walk, which we reached alarmingly close to the top, on down through to meet crowds of excited children. We handed over a rather soggy rabbit to cyclists Rory and Barry McGuire, and prepared to put our feet up at Garve.

Some of the walkers on the way up Ben Wyvis. Suzie Byer, Charge Nurse for the Children's Surgical Ward in Ninewells is in the foreground.
Photo: Mark Tuddenham

Whiteout: Lost on Beinn Dearg

By Jason Hardy – with Simon Crawley

It was only lunchtime on Day One of the Archies Mountain Challenge and Rabbie our cuddly baton had already been cycled from Dingwall to the foot of the first Archie, Ben Wyvis, escorted up and down the mountain by three runners (including my wife, Claire), and was now speeding towards the foot of the second mountain, Beinn Dearg (1064m) by bike. So far I had just been enjoying myself on a nicely paced walk with the children up the lower slopes of Wyvis, but I was due to join Simon Crawley to run up Dearg.

Simon and I left Garve in what we reckoned was good time to get to Loch Droma before cyclists Barry McGuire and his son Rory did, but when we still hadn't caught them by the Aultguish Inn we started to fret. It would not look good to be late for the handover. We needn't have worried – about two kilometres along the side of Loch Glascarnoch we spotted them. Barry, head down pressing on into the wind, Rory on his back wheel trying to make himself as small as possible. The weather was closing in.

We arrived at Loch Droma and met up with Nick in the Archie camper.

'Right lads. All set? Got everything you need? Know where you are going?'

'Yep,' we replied.

'Better get yourselves ready then. They'll be here soon.'

I nipped over the road to check out our starting point. 'Looks pretty straightforward,' I reported back to Simon. 'Through the gateway, then there's a path which we follow north up onto that ridge there. From there we should see the river up to Loch nan Eilean then it's up the southern spur.'

At that point the cyclists arrived and there was a flurry of activity. Greetings made, Rabbie and the all-important GPS tracker handed over and secured in the pack, a few quick shots for *The Adventure Show*, and we were off. After about the first kilometre the path became a stream in a bog, and it was heavy going up to the ridge. From there we descended into a boggy glen with a wide river, the Allt a'Gharbhrain. We spent a few minutes looking for a place to cross before realising that there wasn't one, so we plunged in and forded the river. From the other side it was a steep 600-metre climb up into the cloud, but at least conditions underfoot were dry for the first time.

We reached the summit plateau in a whiteout with visibility less than ten metres. It was snowing and it was difficult to locate the top with map and compass. We had a GPS but it was talking nonsense, so it seemed that our only option was to wander around in the clag. Then we realised we did have another GPS in the form of a tracker in a little rucksack on Rabbie's back, and we had a phone signal. Time to 'phone a friend'!

'Are you watching the tracker?' I asked.

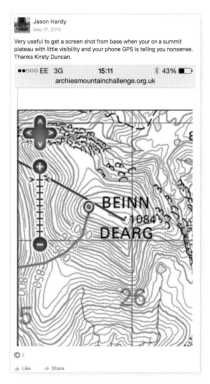

Jason Hardy and Simon Crawley on the summit of Beinn Dearg. Photo: Jason Hardy

'Yes.'

'Where are we? We're on the plateau in zero visibility.'

'You're 200 metres from the summit. Head east.'

Five minutes later we were there. We took a quick summit selfie and set off again. Conditions were not for hanging about in. We descended quickly, skirting the crags, and were soon plunging back through the river, across the bog, and then were soon rewarded with the welcome sight of Nick and the cyclists. Once Rabbie was offloaded and a bowl of hot pasta thrust into our hands, it was time for an interview with *The Adventure Show*.

'So, what happened out there?'

'Simple. We got lost.'

I had the pleasure of driving back out past Beinn Dearg later that evening to pick up the An Teallach runners. At that point the weather had cleared and I was treated to the sun setting behind its summit plateau. Wish it had been like that earlier in the day!

Russell Duncan on An Teallach – Looking south from Sgurr Fiona. Photo: Ben Ulyatt

Forging ahead on the Anvil: An Teallach
By Russell Duncan – with Ben Ulyatt

'This might not be your first Munro – but it will definitely be the finest mountain you've ever climbed.' I tried to impress upon Ben just how much of a privilege it was that we were making our Archie debut on such a magnificent mountain as An Teallach – Gaelic for 'Forge' or 'Anvil' – which hosts the two most northerly of all the Archies. 'This a real belter, Ben, arguably the finest mountain in the whole of the British Isles and certainly in the top ten,' I enthused as we trotted up the north-eastern shoulder of Meall Garbh that carries walkers, runners and climbers onto the bealach that separates Glas Mheall Mor and Bidein a'Ghlas Thuill (1062m).

We had enjoyed watching the clouds and clag clear from its cliffs and ridges for the last 45 minutes and were now close to the top of our first Archie. Fellow walkers on their way down had told us that there was plenty of snow but it was soft and wouldn't pose a problem for two bandits in trainers and Lycra. The depths of the Glas Tholl corrie down to our left were perhaps a wee bit less intimidating than they might have been when not filled with cloud, and as we used all four limbs to reach the summit we realised that it was indeed a little cold. The view of the Atlantic and Summer Isles we had enjoyed over our right shoulders was gone, cloud level being at about one kilometre up! A quick summit selfie with Archie and we were off to Sgurr Fiona (1060m).

The descent was slow because the terrain is real mountain stuff, big-sharp-jaggy stanes, you know the kind, but we got down safely then scampered along to the western approach of Sgurr Fiona where it was back to all fours and a rapid ascent. The top had been shrouded in mist, but when we got there she revealed all of her glories to us in five minutes of wanton abandonment – what a scene unfolded. All of the Archies to the south were clear, and the view over to the Atlantic and beyond. A special moment to savour. Get the picture? Let's get outta here.

The descent from the top is for the surefooted, like the feral goats that live in this part of Scotland, but once you are back in the northern bealach you can scoot swiftly down the old footpath to Dundonnell where your transport may be waiting. Unfortunately for us that meant a quick change of shoes and a pedal up to where Nick and Grant were waiting for us to deliver Rabbie to them for their journey over the kilometre-high Fannaichs.

Night-time adventure: Fannaich Archies
By Grant Rodney – with Nick Leslie

It was my lot to share the final two Archies of the first day of the Challenge with Nick Leslie. I qualified for this rather dubious honour on three counts: first I love hiking in the Scottish hills, second I 'run a bit', and third I am a children's anaesthetist and very closely involved with children's services in NHS Tayside and in helping create their exciting partnership with the ARCHIE Foundation. So, all very well, but to 'run' the Fannaich Archies at night in dubious weather conditions struck me as quite some undertaking. Luckily I was to be accompanied by Nick Leslie, an all-round good guy according to Paul Fettes, and an experienced night-time hill navigator to boot. As well as signing up for this leg, Nick also acted as coordinator for the first week of the Challenge, and was to spend the day in the camper-van-control-vehicle overseeing the numerous Archie legs for that day. We had assembled at the Garve Hotel on Friday night with an air of anticipation and excitement. The Saturday dawned grey, cool but dry, with snow on the hills and more on the way, despite it supposedly being summer in Scotland. Along with some other supporters, I had enjoyed an early morning trip to the Storehouse on the Cromarty Firth to watch the official start, and to enjoy the hospitality with coffee and bacon rolls. One toe dip in the sea later and a bunch of excited cyclists were off, serenaded on their way by a lone piper, paediatric nurse Alison Geddes, and filmed for *The Adventure Show*. From there we all wended our way to the car park at the foot of Ben Wyvis, the first Archie, to witness the handover to the first runners, amid a throng of enthusiastic well-wishers and family walkers of all ages. The starting point was framed by banners, and a couple of ARCHIE gazebos with merchandise, snacks and Challenge T-shirts. After that I spent a relaxing day with colleagues and friends, and enjoying the excitement of the team's progress as the day unfolded.

Finally, it was time to head west and rendezvous with Nick at the start of the Fannaichs ascent, the last leg of the day. It was around 10pm when Russell and Ben appeared on their bikes and we set off. The low cloud had lifted, exposing the An Teallach ridge and the Fannaich hills, and raising the possibility of a moonlit run. Initial going was easy, heading south on a reasonable track alongside the Allt Breabaig. It wasn't long before the track underfoot became a trail of mud and puddles, gradually climbing for a few kilometres as darkness fell. Soon it was time to strike south-east away from the track, heading towards the bealach between Meall a'Chrasgaidh and our first target, Sgurr nan Clach Geala (1093m).

Clouds rolled in and enveloped the moon and sadly that ended the moonlit navigation. It was time for the head torches, with the challenge of uncertain footfall and anticipating the twists and give in the uneven wet vegetation underfoot. We struck upwards beyond the bealach and soon hit the top. A brief pause, obligatory selfie with Archie, energy bar and we were away downhill retracing our steps to the bealach and beyond, while avoiding a steep drop to our right. It was a challenge to find our way in the dark alongside Carn na Criche and beyond, towards Sgurr Mor.

The remaining climb up the great mass of Sgurr Mor (1110m) was a long one, steep and unrelenting. Midnight came and went as we slogged upwards, playing 'guess the

Grant Rodney and Nick Leslie on the Fannaichs. Photo: Nick Leslie

faint footpath', and feeling the cold as the wet seeped into our trail shoes. It was an eerie night-time experience, with visibility restricted to the few misty, murky metres, but it was also exhilarating. We could revel in the simultaneous sensations of solitude and presence: alone at night in the middle of nowhere, but equally surrounded and dwarfed by the bulk of Sgurr Mor and the rest of the Fannaich mountain family. I reflected that, way below at the Garve Hotel, colleagues and friends would be tucked up in bed, after a night of entertainment shared with the coach-party tourists frequenting the hotel, with its quaint rooms, creaking corridors and slightly old-fashioned style of food and entertainment.

We stopped frequently to check our bearings and direction, with me glad of the reassurance of my GPS, but only to confirm the excellence of Nick's traditional navigation skills. Finally, we reached the summit, and savoured the strangely rewarding experience of being perched atop an Archie, after midnight, surrounded by the dank cold and mist.

Another selfie, and it was time for a quadriceps-burning and leg-bracing descent, again requiring frequent stops to check direction. Our head torches cast weird shadows as we made our way back to the original bealach between our two Archies, then steeply downhill to the valley below. It was a little after 2am when we hit the roadside and our vehicles, including Katy Boocock's peaceful camper van, its occupants slumbering ahead of the next day's leg through the Great Wilderness, south to Kinlochewe and beyond.

DAY 2
31 May 2015
4 ARCHIES

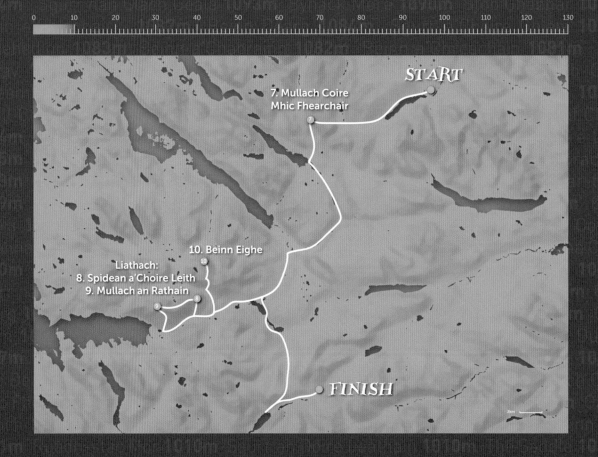

START

7. Mullach Coire
Mhic Fhearchair

10. Beinn Eighe

Liathach:
8. Spidean a'Choire Leith
9. Mullach an Rathain

FINISH

2km

GREAT WILDERNESS
7. Mullach Coire Mhic Fhearchair (1019m): Katy Boocock & Katherine Lawlor. 21km (951m); 7km walk out

MOUNTAIN BIKE OUT
Peter Ferguson. 7km (31m)

ROAD CYCLE
Kinlochewe to Torridon: Barry McGuire & Rory McGuire. 14km (150m)

LIATHACH
8. Spidean a'Choire Leith (1055m), 9. Mullach an Rathain (1023m): David Roberts & Paul Fettes. 8km (1280m)

ROAD CYCLE LINK
Liathach finish to Beinn Eighe start: Barry McGuire & Rory McGuire. 5km (100m)

BEINN EIGHE
10. Ruadh-stac Mor (1010m): Nick Leslie & John Irving. 11km (1090m)

ROAD CYCLE LINK
Paul Fettes. 5km (59m)

MOUNTAIN BIKE TO STRATHCARRON
Barry McGuire & Rory McGuire. 18km (435m)

*Distance in kilometres, (and ascent in metres – this is the cumulative ascent of the leg, even if there is a net descent and the finish is lower than the start). In some cases there was a walk (or run) in or out to the start or finish of a leg without carrying the baton.

Crossing the Great Wilderness
By Katherine Lawlor – with Katy Boocock

A reluctant writer, with the memory capacity of a goldfish, it has come as a surprise to me that, sitting down a year after our Archies Mountain Challenge adventures, I can vividly recall the people and places that I was privileged to encounter.

The Challenge provided an inspiring sense of shared vision and purpose with an ambitious goal, enthusiastic team working and some impressive leadership skills. For two weeks in June the project had the aura of a new cult religion, with the progress of the long eared Rabbie carried so carefully through the high mountains of Scotland being tracked live by avid worshippers on computer screens across the country.

Rabbie's route threaded through the highland landscape, linking up the most beautiful areas of Scotland, fitting together pieces of a jigsaw of ridges, glens and wilderness. As one of the many runners, the joy of the venture was discovering these obscure routes through the mountains, often with a new running partner, and rapidly developing a sense of reliance and trust in someone who an hour or two previously had been a stranger.

I started my Archie adventures with some trepidation. Would I be able to keep up with all these athletic anaesthetists who look so at home in Lycra? Would I get lost (again)? Would I let the team down and put the itinerary back by days? Would I be sucked into a peat bog in the Great Wilderness forever? Would I ever be able to pronounce this mountain's name? These thoughts were pushed aside on the first dawn morning when I had to concentrate on the first navigational challenge – finding my running partner. Katy Boocock was waiting in a camper van in a layby under the Fainnaichs, on the edge of an area known as the Great Wilderness in Wester Ross. We had exchanged a couple of texts and emails but had never met. I was relieved when I knocked on the van's door to find that I was not waking up a hapless tourist. I had passed the first initiative test. Katy, rising bleary-eyed from sleep, seemed quite friendly for that time in the morning and not in the least intimidating. Katy's partner Peter took the obligatory pictures of us with the mascot Rabbie whose innocent childish exterior concealed a James Bond style tracker device. Peter promised to meet us at the other end of our run to speed Rabbie farther on his way by mountain bike.

Katherine Lawlor crossing a stream in the Great Wilderness. Photo: Katy Boocock

We set a reasonable pace along the side of Loch a'Bhraoin, sussing each other out, and settled on a pace which allowed breathing and convivial conversation at the same time. We soon discovered mutual friends and from what I gleaned about Katy, the Challenge was fairly pedestrian compared to some of her previous outdoor antics, including setting up the Strathpuffer, a 24-hour mountain bike event staged in the depths of Scottish midwinter.

We headed up into the mists of our mountain, Mullach Coire Mhic Fhearchair (1019m), with cooperative navigation. I brandished a map and compass but Katy's phone with reassuring satellite-delivered blue dot convinced me that screen time has its place. We picked our route up a grassy slope between slimy rock faces and into a boulder strewn hanging valley. The summit ridge was covered in fine sand, in the mist giving an eerie impression of being back on Broughty Ferry beach, wending our way through the sand dunes. A wet, boggy ridge descent brought us views of Lochan Fada and we trotted along a neatly made cycle path towards Kinlochewe.

The responsibility of keeping Rabbie going at a brisk trot weighed heavily and it was with some relief that we handed him over to Peter, who tore off down the track on his bike. The Great Wilderness was tamed and I had overcome my first-day nerves without recourse to mountain rescue services or helicopters. I considered the day a pretty good initiation to my own personal Archie Challenge.

Looking South the Coulin Pass towards the end of Day 2. Photo: Paul Fettes

Moment of Truth: Liathach
By Paul Fettes – with Dave Roberts

Since I was still recovering from my accident I was exempted any coordinating duties in the first week of the Challenge. The responsibility for allocating people to the various stages was placed onto the shoulders of Nick Leslie and Kirsty Maguire, leaving me to do more simple tasks like run, eat, sleep, repeat, and drink an enormous amount of tea. The arrangement with running was that we would see how things went and I would only do what they and I thought I could cope with.

It was Day Two of the Archie Mountain Challenge, and I was delighted with how it had gone so far. Things had gone to plan yesterday for the Challenge, but also for the family walk which was enjoyed by plenty of folk despite the poor weather. The evening activities had also gone well and there was a really positive vibe. One pleasant surprise was that my wife Heidi and I were on the winning team in the Archie Pub Quiz. I think it is fair to say that we answered our fair share of the questions, but my friend and colleague Craig Cumming (who you will meet later) takes all the credit for our team name 'Whose crazy idea was this anyway?'

I was up for the second run of the day, the first one in Torridon, one of my favourite places. From Kinlochewe the original plan had been a leg over Beinn Eighe, followed by one over Liathach, but the weather forecast suggested severe gales and snow would be arriving during the afternoon, so Nick made the decision that Liathach and its exposed ridge should be tackled first. Excellent. This is a mountain worthy of hyperbole, and a real treat for me. It was also my first mountain run in over a year. Although excited, I was a little concerned about my fitness, and how my legs and particularly my hip would feel. I had been paired up with Dave Roberts, a sub-three-hour marathon runner who had been doing a lot in the hills lately, so I was worried I would be holding him back. Oh well, only one way to find out...

I met Dave on the side of the road in Glen Torridon at around midday. We only had time for a quick hello before the intrepid McGuire duo, Barry and Rory, cycled in from Kinlochewe. We stuffed Rabbie in the top of a sack and set off up the path, which shot straight up the side of the mountain. We chatted breathlessly as we went. I had never met Dave before but found him to be great company. Originally from Dundee, and a good friend of Russell Duncan from school and uni days, he is now a GP in Golspie. A few lung bursting, thigh burning minutes later we were at the top of Spidean a'Choire Leith (1055m). Although we were now in cloud, and were being buffeted by strong winds, we expected a straightforward run westwards along the ridge to Mullach an Rathain (1023m), but on the way there we found ourselves at the top of a precipitous drop. Although it might seem easy to follow a ridge, it is amazing how disorientating it can be when visibility is poor and the cloud is swirling around you. We had come off the main ridge and were left with no option but to retrace our steps until we got back up onto it. We took a careful bearing and set off along what seemed like exactly the same route we had just taken, but this time we found ourselves back on track.

We skipped along the airy ridge to our second summit, and even though there were no views we enjoyed the path as it threaded itself improbably through the spectacular, ancient rock architecture of the Fasarinen Pinnacles. Then as we descended on a steep rocky path with some fairly treacherous scree sections, the cloud cleared and we could savour views of the ridge as we descended. Soon we could see vehicles and the bionic McGuires at the roadside, ready for a short cycle up the glen.

Our final stretch was a flat section spattered with bog myrtle and bog cotton, so I suppose I should not have been surprised when I found myself thigh deep in watery peat in full sight of the others! With handover duties completed, we watched Nick and John disappear up Beinn Eighe. Barry and Rory then had a couple of hours before they were needed for the last section of the day, a cracking mountain bike ride south to Strathcarron, so we all headed back to Kinlochewe for some well-earned down time at the Tipsy Laird café, and some impromptu generosity – like many others on the way, when the owner heard what we were doing she gave us a donation.

Beinn Eighe
By John Irving - with Nick Leslie

Katherine (Lawlor) and I met as students in the Edinburgh University Mountaineering Club, and have tried to maintain similar hill interests as time and opportunities become scarce. We try to divide things evenly, but it doesn't always work out fair. During my glory leg up Ben Wyvis, she had cajoled the kids into the mist, but we all enjoyed the Garve Hotel pub games. Sunday morning, I had a lie in, she got up at 4:30 for a run across the Great Wilderness to Kinlochewe. She got wind and rain, I enjoyed a short walk with the kids over the Corrieshalloch Gorge, before we all had a pub lunch in Kinlochewe.

I met the Challenge camper van at the layby in Glen Torridon, and sorted out the route up Beinn Eighe over fresh coffee. Nick was keen to jog round the path into Coire Mhic Fhearchair, but I managed to persuade him that the direct line up the scree would be much more efficient. In the event, and despite the forecast, the weather was kind to us. We nipped up and down in blustery sunshine and the odd snow shower, talking of mutual acquaintances and student days. On the top we skimmed round the edge of the magnificent cliffs to the tenth Archie summit of the weekend, Ruadh-stac Mor (1010m). From there it was back down the way we came, to hand over to Paul who gave Rabbie a short spin along the road before handing him on to Barry and Rory, who sped off on their mountain bikes. A steady grind up to the Coulin Pass was followed by an exhilarating descent to Achnashellach where activities were put on 'pause' until the following morning. Rabbie was then whisked off to Achnasheen where the team enjoyed some late and great bar food in the grandeur of Ledgowan Lodge.

Top and bottom – John Irving on Beinn Eighe. Photos: Nick Leslie

DAY 3
1 June 2015
5 ARCHIES

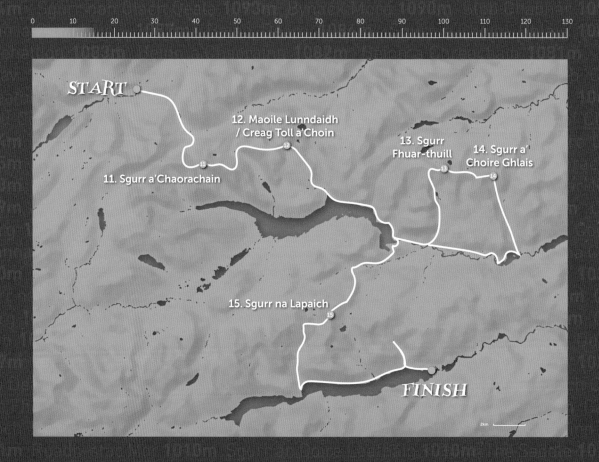

START

12. Maoile Lunndaidh
/ Creag Toll a'Choin

13. Sgurr
Fhuar-thuill

14. Sgurr a'
Choire Ghlais

11. Sgurr a'Chaorachain

15. Sgurr na Lapaich

FINISH

2km

ACHNASHELLACH TO MONAR LODGE

11. Sgurr a'Chaorachain (1053m), 12. Maoile Lunndaidh / Creag Toll a'Choin (1005m): Kirsty Maguire & Elspeth Luke. 25km (1025m)

ROAD CYCLE

Paul Fettes. 4km (60m)

STRATHFARRAR HILLS

13. Sgurr Fhuar-thuill (1049m), 14. Sgurr a'Choire Ghlais (1083m): Katy Boocock & Jason Hardy. 14km (1140m)

ROAD CYCLE

Paul Fettes. 14km (360m)

MONAR TO MULLARDOCH

15. Sgurr na Lapaich (1150m) Two aborted (An Riabhachan, An Socach): Nick Leslie & Katherine Lawlor. 24km (1590m)

*Distance in kilometres, (and ascent in metres – this is the cumulative ascent of the leg, even if there is a net descent and the finish is lower than the start). In some cases there was a walk (or run) in or out to the start or finish of a leg without carrying the baton.

Trip to Narnia: Achnashellach to Monar Lodge
By Kirsty Maguire – with Elspeth Luke

'I've been here before,' I said with some trepidation. 'This car park was the worst soggy, midge infested and dark camping spot I've ever experienced.' A vaguely preoccupied, and not entirely surprised, Elspeth glanced sideways at me, with a 'you probably brought it on yourself' look. When we'd been sitting in Paul's kitchen in Dundee planning this trip, I'd been imagining long, dry sunshine filled summer days – the best that Scotland has to offer, in fact. Crisp mountain air, a light breeze to keep the midges away and long days running fleet of foot through brittle springy heather and into the short starlit night.

Instead, we had sheeting rain, a slate grey sky and in my half-asleep state, when getting out of my cosy bed at about 3:30am in Achnasheen, I'd mistaken an entirely snow cloaked mountain outside for a white fluffy cloud. It's June. Snow isn't for June. Time to pull out those shiny new 'winter mountaineering' bits of kit I'd bought in the sale in February and put away for next winter.

Pleased to leave my least favourite camping spot, we set off up the forest track near Achnashellach station, past the sleeping construction site of a new hydro scheme and up the river Allt a'Chonais. We'd got the early shift run this morning, and as cousins and frequent running partners, the politeness of strangers was replaced by comedy jibes. The first climb on still sleeping limbs was trudged through, but soon we were trotting along with the rhythmic swoosh swoosh of waterproofs, as the rain was drumming down on our hoods, keeping us in our own mini worlds. However, both of us were nervously eyeing the raging torrent of a river on our right and looking for the wire bridge.

After an initial failed attempt to cross, we found the right bridge and edged unstably across, keen not to take a dip. Smiling at making it over that river, we headed confidently along the path to find... hang on, this river is a stream on the map! Pacing up and down the bank for some time looking a bit baffled and reluctant, we eventually managed to cross safely. River crossings aren't usually something I've had to think about much before in Scotland despite playing in the hills most weekends. Admittedly this is the type of day we'd usually choose a long lie, a low-level run, and

Sgurr a'Chaorachain. Photo: Kirsy Maguire

a trip to a warm pub, but somehow the day was becoming enjoyable. OK, Type 2 fun perhaps so far, but that's certainly significantly better than Type 3.

At 450m we moved into a different world. Knee-deep drifting powder snow and icy toes in our river-soaked hill-running shoes. We stopped behind a small boulder so Elspeth could add some more layers. Just as she had her bag open and kit out, a squall came through, blowing the dry snow into everything. Winter was toying with us. Laughing the laugh of the slightly mad, we kept on going. The wind was getting up and the horizontal hail was scrubbing our faces. I kept dreaming wistfully of the snow goggles I'd left in the cupboard at home thinking 'surely I won't need those'. The summit cairn on Sgurr a'Chaorachain (1053m) swam out of the cloud soon enough. We huddled down and took the obligatory summit photo with Rabbie the Archie rabbit. The photo shows us grimacing and trying to look as though there is nowhere we would rather be. It also shows blurry horizontal white streaks of blown snow. Bracing!

Taking a bearing to stay on the ridge and avoid the north-east wind-slab-laden snow slopes, we set off downhill, enjoying running through the soft snow. Engrossed in following the bearing in a whiteout I didn't notice the wind easing off until it had gone. We ran out of the cloud and were faced with the most stunning view. White as far as we could see, blue sky and sunshine. It was like we'd been released from our own tiny worlds inside the waterproofs and transported to Narnia. No wardrobe to step through, a storm cloud instead. Whooping with joy and excitement we took some photos and kept running down through the deep snow. Soaked to the skin from the waists down already and buoyed by the stunning scenery, the bog hidden under the snow was a mere technicality.

Up and over Maoile Lunndaidh and its twin peak Creag Toll a'Choin (1005m) and down a long wet slope to Loch Monar, the sun continued to shine and the early morning grimness seemed a world away. The lochside path was nicely runnable and from some distance away we could see Monar Lodge, where our reception committee and Paul on a bike awaited. Soggy and hungry, but smiling, we arrived and handed over.

Enjoying some down-time in Glen Strathfarrar

Having joined the Challenge two days after it started, Glen Strathfarrar was my first opportunity to experience the event complexities. We'd spent months helping Paul to plan the route and I had been imagining it in my mind's eye, but with the weather conditions, immensely complicated logistics and ever changing group of enthusiastic and hugely experienced hill people, seeing the reality of the ARCHIE beast in action was impressive.

The time spent in vans meeting and speaking to people, planning, and sharing stories of other adventures was entirely immersive and really inspiring. Between run legs I snatched conversations with people that I hadn't met before, but who I would soon find popping up in random laybys in the most remote parts of Scotland, and at all times of day and night (despite there being no way of communicating with them directly due to lack of phone or internet). They all seemed to be overflowing with enthusiasm, and have vehicles filled with kit and bristling with bikes and kayaks. It was truly amazing. Just when we thought we were lacking someone with particular skills, they would appear as if by magic having driven across the country through the night.

Glen Strathfarrar – Katy Boocock and Jason Hardy with Rabbie. Photos: Jason Hardy

Giant steps on the Strathfarrar hills
By Jason Hardy – with Katy Boocock

Having got a bit lost on Beinn Dearg on the first day I was keen to redeem myself
on the two Archies in Glen Strathfarrar. For those who haven't been there, Glen
Strathfarrar can only be accessed via a locked gate, which is possible to have
unlocked if you ask nicely in advance. It's a fantastic drive up the glen – the road
snakes its way up between the hills and there were large herds of red deer grazing
by the river. At the head of the glen is Loch Monar and Monar Lodge where I met up
with fellow Archie athletes. When runners Kirsty Maguire and Elspeth Luke appeared
at the side of the lodge, they passed Rabbie on to Paul who cycled down the Glen
to the point where Katy Boocock and I duly set off up Sgurr Fhuar-thuill (1049m). We
made good progress up the Allt Toll a'Mhuic path and it wasn't until we climbed the
path out of the corrie that we realised how much shelter we had been getting from
the wind. We were back to true June Archie bagging weather – mist, sleet and a gale!

With little reason to hang about we made quick progress along the ridge, only stopping briefly for summit selfies and a short Rabbie video clip. Once over Sgurr a'Choire Ghlais (1083m) we descended quickly back down to the glen over a strange geographical quirk – giant steps on the side of the hill which are apparently kame terraces, a product of the glaciation which shaped this land many moons ago. At one point our descent was more rapid than expected, down a steep wet grassy bank. First Katy and then I slipped, rapidly picking up speed and smashing into a snow bank at the bottom. Having dusted ourselves off and awarded each other marks for artistic impression, we made our way back out to the road to rendezvous with the others. We passed Rabbie back to Paul who was ready on his bike to take him on his next adventure.

Winter demons: Scoured off Sgurr na Lapaich
By Nick Leslie and Katherine Lawlor

Nick: When one of my best and longest-standing friends told me about his idea for the Challenge, my immediate thoughts were that I would love to be involved. It was a great idea that could raise a lot of money for charity, and I could have fun running round the Highlands with my friends in the process. I immediately offered my help as Challenge dogsbody, driver, planner and runner. I also generously offered to drink beer and eat pasta whenever anyone needed me to! Even better, we could pick the time of year and do it in early summer – it was bound to be gorgeous.

So, on the 1st June about a year later, I was heading up Sgurr na Lapaich from Glen Strathfarrar with Katherine. It was early afternoon, it was raining, worse was forecast and pretty soon we'd be heading into the clouds. I had a small runner's rucksack packed with some spare kit, food, blizzard pack survival bag, head torch, a mobile phone and a GPS unit strapped to a decent sized cuddly cloth rabbit. It was Day Three of the Challenge and so far things had gone pretty well (and to plan) for everyone, despite some bad weather. Personally, I'd enjoyed a lovely midnight trot over the Fannaichs with Grant Rodney and a very windy but dry and fun whizz up Beinn Eighe with Katherine's husband, John Irving.

Katherine: Full of optimism after my successful run with Katy over the Great Wilderness, I set off with Nick to link up Glen Strathfarrar with Glen Cannich across the ridge that separates these two remote glens. We had not met before, but the Archie Challenge had a unique way of throwing people together and encouraging storming, forming, and action without too much need for introductions and social niceties. We set off up the slopes from Loch Monar at a tremendous pace, which did not seem to stem the chat at all and led me to revise my sexist belief that blokes don't talk. The slopes on our way up the hill offered us protection from the prevailing wind so that the ascent was warm and benign, and despite rain and poor visibility we found ourselves on top of Sgurr na Lapaich (1150m) in what seemed like no time at all. We took some summit selfies and had a lively debate about preferred navigation techniques as we headed westwards along the ridge towards An Riabhachan.

Nick: A cold wind had picked up and the heavy rain had long since turned to snow. I was expecting a long run in the wind and snow and I've had plenty of those, so I wasn't too concerned. I munched a chewy bar and put on my gloves and last spare fleece. Visibility was short, maybe twenty or thirty metres, and although mid-afternoon meant plenty of daylight left, the wind across the ridge was cold and buffeting, with fresh snow filling the spaces between the rocks. Despite wearing all my clothes, I was starting to feel very cold and wet. The kit I had chosen at

Nick Leslie checking the map in Glen Strathfarrar as we wait for Jason and Katy. Photo: Katherine Lawlor

home whilst thinking about bad days running in the hills was still running kit after all, and I had a strong feeling that my trusty yellow waterproof might be breaching its definition. I was getting into a trudge-on survival mode, just following Katherine through the windy whiteness. The conditions meant there was no way of talking – even a shout was lost in the wind – and the shape of the ridge forced us to walk exposed to the worst of the wind to avoid the precipitous northern crag edges.

Katherine: My initial optimism waned as we headed west into driving, icy rain and strong winds. As we made further progress, rain turned to blizzard and there was plenty of snow, fuelling concerns about avalanches. We began to have difficulty remaining upright and steering clear of the ugly black drops disappearing into the swirling abyss on the north side of the ridge. Constantly battered by the wind, disorientated by painful needles of snow in our eyes, we had to shout to be heard above the noise of the gale. Arriving at a narrow section of the ridge, frozen fingers gripped the rocks, feet slipped on the snow and now and then we sank into drifts up to our knees. We found some welcome shelter behind a boulder, relieved to be out of the raw wind, and shared out all our spare clothes and choked down some chocolate rations. Nick's teeth were chattering but he was ominously quiet. It was difficult to know what he was thinking. Was this uncharacteristic reticence due to the onset of hypothermia or was he just fed up? We studied the map. We were pretty near our next Archie, however beyond this was a narrow stretch of ridge, likely to be snarled up with snow. The map indicated further precipitous cliffs. The experience of the last few metres had been unnerving, unbalanced by the unrelenting wind, feet slipping with vertiginous glimpses of plunging vertical rock faces. This was not what happens on a summer day in June.

Nick: After an hour or so in the blizzard, I was having to put in extra efforts just to keep up, so we waved each other towards the northern lee of a rare sheltering rock, huddling close enough to speak. We ate some food and Katherine gave me her last spare layer, a thin duvet jacket which made me feel better for a few minutes. I was amazed she wasn't already wearing everything she carried. She seemed almost chipper, and in as good a state as someone could be in those conditions, but I was cold and struggling. We knew we couldn't carry on for another hour or two to An Socach at the western end of the ridge, but we were within a few hundred metres of An Riabhachan so we agreed to try to go on, at least that far.

Katherine: My mountain demons were returning with thoughts of a fateful hill walk one winter when a straightforward day out turned into something quite different. The day climaxed by being plucked unceremoniously off the hill, spinning into space in the dark, being winched upwards towards the deafening noise and downdraft from the blades of a helicopter above. That day's experience, the result of a series of my own navigational errors, an over-ambitious route choice for the party's abilities and suboptimal communication, left me chastened and dented my mountain confidence for a while afterwards. A remedial navigation course and several mountain marathons later had seen my mountain mojo return but this was not a situation I wanted to repeat. On the ridge with Nick, I had the same sickening feeling of plans unravelling and the situation beginning to spin out of control. Our designated task was to knock off some Archies and deliver Rabbie safely to the next runners so that the Archie Challenge could continue. If we did not succeed we would let the whole team down, scupper the schedule and risk the disappointment and ridicule of our peers. The thought of jacking it all in was galling but then the idea of making a mistake and turning the Archie Challenge into a newspaper headline for all the wrong reasons was also not an appealing one. The tracker was on, and we were being watched, Big-Brother-like, by people at home. We simply had to keep going.

Nick: Restarting, the uphill gradient soon increased and, although visibility remained poor, we were pretty confident we were very close to the summit. However, the snow was slippery, hard and steep enough that without an ice axe, or clear sight of what lay above and below, we couldn't safely climb it. We didn't speak, but there was no doubt about the agreed message.

Katherine: Gesticulating wildly to one another over the gale, I think we were both relieved to be pointing towards our escape route, heading down a southerly slope out of the unrelenting wind and away from the threatening cliffs. The nagging doubts about avalanches were swept away as we careened down the snow slope and gratefully reached the reassuring grass tussocks beyond.

Out of the wind and driving rain and moving quickly again, we soon warmed up and our brains began functioning more normally. It was with new eyes and heightened senses that we viewed the landscape of rivers in full spate, great noises of rushing water leaping into the air, blown upwards by the howling wind. Feet remained numb but the sodden brown grass was a welcome change from the piercing cold whites and greys of the summit ridge. This now felt like a familiar day out on the hill, back to a reassuring level of virtuous discomfort.

Nick: Snow gave way to sleet, then rain, weakening by the time we got to the western end of Loch Mullardoch, about an hour after leaving the ridge. I think we were both feeling pretty low, only gradually talking more as we slowed and neared the loch. There was a mix of knowing we couldn't have carried on to complete our intended route safely, and that an accident would really ruin the Challenge. On the other hand, we also realised how much plans would need to change and others would need to run to get the two missing summits. I felt slightly better from the sincerity with which Katherine said she couldn't or wouldn't have gone on either, but in my mind I had been the one struggling most.

Katherine: We trudged back along Loch Mullardoch on paths ankle deep in water, sneaking occasional glances upwards towards the ridge, reassuring each other that we had made the right decision not to press on. By that time, the ridge had cleared and it glimmered white in the evening sunshine, mocking us for our ignoble retreat. Had we imagined the conditions up there? Had I let my mountain demons get the better of us?

Nick: It took about three hours to get back along Loch Mullardoch to the waiting camper, in what became a nice evening with a sunset behind us. We were both tired but safe, and only slightly annoyed at the 250m re-ascent required to cross safely over the last burn-turned-raging-torrent before the eastern end of the loch. Paul was waiting in the van in the gathering darkness, and having been without phone signal took news of our troubles well.

Katherine: Back with a big steaming bowl of pasta, and a hot drink in the warm fug of the Archiemobile camper van Paul was careful not to make us feel guilty about our aborted mission. The main thing was that we were safe, and he revised the plans so that the peaks we had missed out would be attempted again the following day.

Nick: In retrospect, it was one of my most memorable days in the hills, mostly for the wrong reasons – experiencing what would have been bad blizzard conditions for January when it was actually June. I guess without a schedule to stick to and others relying on it, there is no way that we would have planned a long ridge run with such a windy and wintery forecast.

Nick Leslie crossing a raging torrent that should be a burbling burn. Photo: Katherine Lawlor

In front of the stove, Broughty Ferry
By John Irving (Katherine's husband)

Monday evening, home after a big paperwork day. The weather blattered at the windows just like a winter gale – a good excuse to light the wood stove. The tracker updated irregularly. Katherine and Nick were out on Sgurr na Lapaich. They seemed to stick for a while below the summit, then jump over to the col beyond. Three more updates and they were well on their way to the second Archie, An Riabhachan, after which there would be a relatively short skip and a hop to the third, An Socach, before turning away from the wind and jogging down to the shore of the loch and back to the dam. The tracker jumped to an odd location south of the ridge, and stopped. The remains of the tea went cold, the planned administration faded from attention. The rational explanation of poor signal, or weak battery power in the cold and rain lost conviction. A throwaway remark on Facebook about avalanches stopped seeming impossible. The fire burnt down. Then the tracker jumped to the lochshore, and all was well.

DAY 4
2 June 2015
5 ARCHIES

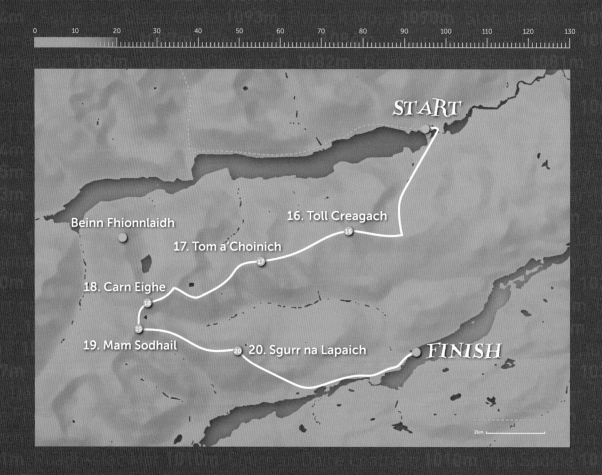

START

16. Toll Creagach

Beinn Fhionnlaidh

17. Tom a'Choinich

18. Carn Eighe

19. Mam Sodhail

20. Sgurr na Lapaich

FINISH

2km

MULLARDOCH HILLS

Two aborted (An Riabhachan, An Socach): Barry McGuire & Matthew Mccullagh. 22km (1070m)

SHORT ROAD CYCLE LINK

Paul Fettes. 2km (50m)

NORTH AFFRIC

CARN EIGHE HORSESHOE. 16. Toll Creagach (1054m), 17. Tom a'Choinich (1112m), 18. Carn Eighe (1183m), 19. Mam Sodhail (1181m), 20. Sgurr na Lapaich (1036m): Paul Fettes & Elspeth Luke. 25km (1810m)

*Distance in kilometres, (and ascent in metres – this is the cumulative ascent of the leg, even if there is a net descent and the finish is lower than the start). In some cases there was a walk (or run) in or out to the start or finish of a leg without carrying the baton.

The Best Laid Schemes o' Mice an' Men
By Matthew McCullagh – with Barry McGuire

'Twas a dark and stormy night when we drove north from Perth, heading to a small hostelry west of Inverness, in preparation for an early start the following morning. The plan was to meet up with Paul and crew at the Loch Mullardoch dam at 05:45, grab Rabbie, trot over a few Archies on the Carn Eighe horseshoe, hand over to the next runners in Glen Affric and then have kippers for breakfast – well, something like that anyway. But, as the other Rabbie says, 'schemes... gang aft agley...'

In reality, we woke at 05:00 to a satellite text message from Paul saying that we wouldn't be running our planned route as things hadn't quite gone to plan the previous evening, but still to meet at the same rendezvous point. We arrived to find the Archie camper van but no sign of life. A hoot of our horn brought a sleepy face to the van window – not the sort of face that only a mother could love, but certainly one that a mother would want to iron, riddled as it was with the creases of a night in a sleeping bag. In the van we were greeted with the gentle aroma of damp 'Smelly Hansens', and watched as other faces appeared from the most unlikely places (Paul seemed to have slept in a glove compartment above the driver's seat).

We heard how Katherine and Nick had been unable to bag the last two Archies on their route. Our brief was therefore to go back up and bag these before the team could continue on its planned way. To say we were disappointed is an understatement – we now had no real idea where we were going and the route in along the loch shoreline to our peaks was described as 'brutal'.

The Archies we were heading for were An Riabhachan and the more distant An Socach. Despite being advised to head for An Socach first, we decided to make our way towards An Riabhachan from the south side. The initial five kilometres were very boggy and the landscape was riddled with peat hags. Anything to get off this trudgery had seemed like a good plan but, in hindsight, heading up the nearer hill may have been unwise. As we climbed it got colder and at about 1000m we entered the cloud and experienced poor visibility, deep snow and smooth, white, featureless terrain. A break in the cloud allowed us to see a steep, snooker-ball-smooth snowfield and what looked like a serious cornice waiting for us on the summit ridge. We had no ice axes or crampons with us, were both wearing hill running shoes and felt seriously under-equipped for the conditions. Our worry was that even if we didn't trigger an avalanche (and the risk must have been pretty high), if we slipped on the snow we wouldn't be able to stop ourselves sliding downhill and potentially over the crags littered below us. We spent what seemed like a lifetime debating options, but really there was little to debate.

We were desperate to bag our Archies but we were also mindful that the Challenge was supposed to be an enjoyable event and that no-one would thank us for throwing in a couple of hospital cases (although it would have got us some publicity, and 'there is no such thing as bad publicity'). What made it worse was the realisation that if we couldn't get to the first Archie, we would have no way of getting to the second as the ridge was almost certainly too dangerous. With heavy hearts (and heavy socks, gloves and hats) we headed back down to the Mullardoch lochside and began a nine-kilometre muddy trudge back to the van.

Returning to the others waiting in the van after 6½ hours with neither Archie bagged was very difficult (we had to watch their faces change from glee to tempered disappointment), but everyone was very supportive and agreed that we had made the right decision. Nick Leslie aided our recovery by filling us with hot food and warm encouragement – if ever he fancies a career change I'm pretty sure he could walk into a job as a chef in a (Pot) noodle bar!

Make or Break: The Carn Eighe Horseshoe
By Paul Fettes – with Elspeth Luke

Elspeth and I were pretty much ready for our run over the Carn Eighe horseshoe when Matthew and Barry arrived back in what seemed like very good time. We were delighted to see them, but our initial excitement turned rapidly to dismay when they told us they had failed in their quest. The Challenge was in danger of unravelling, and grinding to a halt. Clearly access to An Riabhachan and An Socach was difficult from the east when they were this packed with snow. We could have stayed and debriefed with Matthew and Barry for a while, but it wasn't going to help us complete the Challenge. I had no doubt they had made the right decision to bail out and safety was of paramount importance, but now we had to decide what to do next. It didn't seem worth going back for a third attempt, but if we headed south to Glen Affric then it would be a long way back to try to reach those remote peaks again from this side.

'Nick, can we get to those hills from the west on another day?' I asked (he had planned this section of the Challenge).

'Yes,' was the immediate reply, 'you can access them from Kintail on a good track, although it's a long way in.'

'OK. Well, in that case I think Elspeth and I should head south. We can head up Toll Creagach and play it by ear from there.'

A quick look at the map confirmed that it should be straightforward to head south to Glen Affric off our first hill. The same looked likely from the next summit, Tom a'Choinich, so we agreed that we would aim to 'bag' one or possibly two hills and probably head down from there. Only if things were really looking good would we go for the full horseshoe. A quick peanut-butter-and-honey sandwich and a milky coffee and I was ready for almost anything. From where we were perched high on the north side of the dam, it would have made sense to run along the top of the dam, except the middle section was impassable and we had no option but to go down the road and up the other side. That would be quicker on a bike, so I set off with a large unwieldy camper van in hot pursuit.

From the south side of the dam, Elspeth and I followed a little footpath threading its way through a feeble copse of pine trees. After that the path led out on to heather and gradually petered out. We chatted as we made our way up in the shelter of the north-east corrie, aiming to hit the east ridge a fair bit below the summit, where the snow looked reasonably thin. I hadn't met Elspeth before apart from in passing the day before, but one of the pleasures of this challenge was spending time with like-minded and likeable people.

Elspeth is Kirsty Maguire's cousin. She is also an ultra-runner, and at the time she was in training for a big challenge that summer. I think this was part of the reason that Kirsty had roped her in, and probably part of the reason she had agreed. Her aim was to run the watershed of Scotland, up the spine of the country from south to north.

She was inspired to do this after reading Peter Wright's book *Ribbon of Wildness*, and planned to raise money for a Parkinson's disease charity because her Dad had recently been diagnosed with the condition. This struck a chord with me because my Dad also has Parkinson's. I thought it unlikely that my Dad would qualify for or benefit from the surgical treatment she mentioned, but it certainly sounded a worthwhile aspiration and cause.

As we crested the ridge we were greeted as expected by a cold wind, but it wasn't as fierce or as biting as I had feared. We headed up an easy incline to the summit in driving snow, and as we approached my phone started pinging manically. I now had contact with the outside world for the first time in about 48 hours. (This wasn't strictly true – we did have a satellite phone in the van, but it was a very basic model, difficult to use, and you had to be outside to get any hope of reception, so while it worked after a fashion for sending texts, we didn't seem to receive any.) I received several texts from a rather concerned Heidi, miscellaneous stuff about the Challenge, one rather bizarrely from my bank, and a real cracker from Russell:

> Well I can honestly say that Kirsty and I were on the edge of our seats as we watched you try to negotiate those torrents in spate last night Nick. It made for great drama but I've no doubt it was a grim experience and hope you are all still hale and hearty this morning.

It seemed pretty unlikely that there was CCTV in this remote area, so I took this to mean that they had been following the progress of the tracker online. It seemed both ironic and surreal that while we were battling the elements in our own little isolation bubble, interested parties potentially all over the globe could follow our antics from the comfort and safety of their own homes. In fact, some of them had been held spellbound. I did not consider answering the texts. We were on a remote mountain in pretty inhospitable conditions and we didn't want to hang around for any longer than we had to. From the summit of Toll Creagach (1054m), we could see the grey bulk of Tom a'Choinich (1112m) looming out of the gloom.

At this point we still were not sure what to do. The safest option was to bail out and head south off the hill to a warm, waiting camper van in Glen Affric, but after a brief discussion we agreed to head on to the second hill. It was only mid-afternoon and there was still plenty of daylight. We were both warm and had plenty of food. As we ran over hard-crusted snow interspersed with patches of black heather, the clouds cleared to give us a good view of the next hill, and seemed to vindicate our decision. Rather than take a large detour on snow-free ground, I suggested taking the beeline, straight up a little ridge of black on the east face of the mountain. There was a large nose of snow at the top, but it looked passable. There was no cornice above it and I was confident we could make it up.

We made good progress up the little ridge. At the top, the nose of snow looked passable with care, and we took our axes out of our bags. Elspeth was clearly quite scared at this point, but I coaxed her up. I made sure that she knew how to use the axe as a brake, and although it was actually possible to kick steps, I also showed her how you could use the axe to help cut steps in the crusty snow without using too much energy – something climber Tom Patey had shown my Dad many moons ago. Soon the incline became gentler, and as we trotted to the top I congratulated Elspeth on overcoming her fear of the climb. We were now on the summit of Tom a'Choinich, and were faced with another decision – either head along the snowy ridge of the horseshoe, or head down towards Affric. The ridge south of the summit looked straightforward, but the way forward looked inviting. The ground was hard and pretty runnable, and the weather was better than it had been. The problem was that if we went any farther there would be no backing out. The ground on either side of the ridge was laden with snow. There was no halfway house. It was either go all the way round the horseshoe, or back the way we had come. I was conscious of the potential for disaster here, but we were warm, the wind had eased off a little, we had plenty of daylight left, and plenty of food and water. Weighing it up we made what we felt was a rational decision to go on.

From the back of my mind, another concern reared its ugly head. Although I was making a good recovery from my head injury, was I really able to think straight? Was I really mentally competent to make sensible decisions? Was it possible that I could be prone to lapses in concentration and mental fatigue? I could not dismiss these questions, but I felt invigorated and alert, and I did not share them with Elspeth. I made the unilateral decision that I was in a good enough state to continue.

We carried on in a white world. The sky was white, and there was fresh snow all around us. It was hard to credit the fact that it was nearly midsummer. Although any path there might have been was hidden by snow we made good progress, finding a safe way past the pinnacles of An Leth-chreag and along a thin ridge to the main body of Carn Eighe (1183m). By this time the weather was closing in and we reached the top in blizzard conditions at 6pm.

Although really delighted with our progress, navigation was tricky in poor visibility, and I was worried about getting safely off the mountain. To the north of Carn Eighe there was an outlier from the horseshoe, Beinn Fhionnlaidh, but in my mind it would have been crazy to attempt that. It was a 'no brainer' to head for home. We found a good line up Mam Sodhail (1181m) and as we made our way down off the summit, we came out of the cloud and could see the ridge leading to Sgurr na Lapaich (1036m) in front of us. The reduction in altitude also meant less snow and although we were both getting tired (at least I certainly was) we made good progress to our last Archie of the day. Although it was steep in places, the descent was safe enough and we made good time glissading down some huge snow patches.

The long weary run out was made easier by the beauty of Glen Affric and its Scots Pine forest, and by the feeling of elation that we had completed a pretty challenging section safely, despite the hostile conditions. A pair of camper vans in a layby on the road was an extremely welcome sight, as were we to the inhabitants.

I am amused by how many people have since asked me why we didn't do Beinn Fhionnlaidh. 'You have no idea what it was like up there' just doesn't seem to do it justice.

Elspeth had planned to head south that evening for work the next day, but in the event she decided to stay with friends near Inverness. In the morning rather than drive home to Glasgow, she drove to Edinburgh where, as a professional musician she was due to teach music. On the way there she called in at a clothes shop to buy some work attire. Ironically, after all her effort to make it on time, her first two lessons were cancelled!

A few weeks later, on the 22nd August 2015, Elspeth completed her 680-mile Scottish Watershed Run from Peel Fell in the Borders to Duncansby Head on the north coast. She took 34 days and raised £14,255 for 'Funding Neuro' in the process. You can read about it in her blog: watershedscotland.blogspot.uk.

DAY 5
3 June 2015
7 ARCHIES

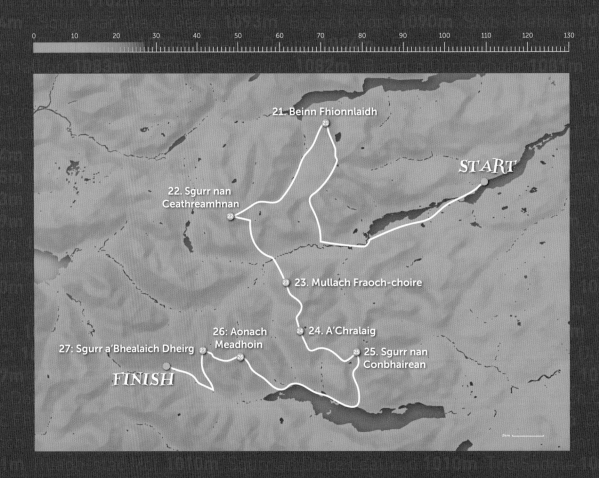

21. Beinn Fhionnlaidh

START

22. Sgurr nan Ceathreamhnan

23. Mullach Fraoch-choire

24. A'Chralaig

26: Aonach Meadhoin

27: Sgurr a'Bhealaich Dheirg

25. Sgurr nan Conbhairean

FINISH

NORTH AFFRIC: OUTLIERS

21. Beinn Fhionnlaidh (1005m), 22. Sgurr nan Ceathreamhnan (1151m): Katherine Lawlor & Kirsty Maguire. Mountain bike 12 km, (260m), Run 25km (2070m), cycle out 15km.

AFFRIC TO KINTAIL

23. Mullach Fraoch-choire (1102m), 24. A'Chralaig (1120m), 25: Sgurr nan Conbhairean (1109m): Gary Mooney & Nick Leslie. 15km (1450m) after 15km cycle in.

ROAD CYCLE LINK

Paul Fettes. 6km (80m)

CLUANIE DUO

26: Aonach Meadhoin (1001m), 27: Sgurr a'Bhealaich Dheirg (1036m): Ben Ulyatt & Paul Fettes. 9km (1070m)

ROAD CYCLE LINK

Nick Leslie. 5km (30m)

*Distance in kilometres, (and ascent in metres – this is the cumulative ascent of the leg, even if there is a net descent and the finish is lower than the start). In some cases there was a walk (or run) in or out to the start or finish of a leg without carrying the baton.

Beinn Fhionnlaidh and Sgurr nan Ceathreamhnan from Glen Affric

By Katherine Lawlor – with Kirsty Maguire

Kirsty and I did not know each other before the Challenge but paired up as a running team for two legs. Exploring new places together while getting to know one another were positive and rewarding aspects of the adventure. It appealed to my feminist principles that the girls got a chance to join in with the mountain capers and contribute to the success of the Challenge.

Following my day with Nick when we were scoured off Sgurr na Lapaich by blizzards, I was hoping for a more straightforward trip. Our first route took us from Glen Affric up a collection of hills forming a band between Loch Mullardoch in Glen Cannich in the north and Loch Affric to the south. As someone with a poor sense of geography it was very illuminating for me to link up these remote glens by travelling between them in a linear route, so partly completing the jigsaw of the Highlands. Our mountain hit-list for the day included Beinn Fhionnlaidh (1005m) and Sgurr nan Ceathreamhnan (1151m), which are an unlikely pairing in any guidebook since they are separated by nine kilometres and 1000m ascent. There were several peaks on the way, the summits of which we scorned as they were not on our itinerary. This would raise an eyebrow from any keen Munro bagger, but part of the charm of the Challenge was taking the unconventional approach and the path less travelled.

We set off from the luxury of the Archiemobile camper van at an early hour shortly after dawn – and this really is early during a Scottish midsummer when it is dark for only a few hours. Glen Affric has a wild timeless beauty with its ancient forests of Scots Pine. Cycling along the lochside through the tranquil woodland, the valley opened up before us, green and inviting. Finding the right spot to stash our bikes, we headed up hill on foot. Negotiating a steady pace which suited us both we followed an old drove path beside a meandering river, and up the glen to Bealach Coire Ghaidheil. This track links two remote glens, and progressing pilgrim-like along it created a sense that we were following a route walked by centuries of travellers.

We took a rising traverse towards Mam Sodhail and on towards Beinn Fhionnlaidh. The mist came down and the cold increased. An uncomfortable feeling of déjà vu descended too.

Kirsty Maguire coming off Sgurr nan Ceathreamhnan. Photo: Katherine Lawlor

Unhelpful negative thoughts regarding previous map reading errors and helicopters resurfaced. However, Kirsty remained optimistic and our exemplary map reading led us to an old roofless stone shelter where we escaped the wind and took stock. Morale improved with cake, as is often the case, and we trotted on to Beinn Fhionnlaidh, passing over a snow bridge across a stream, taking photos which would look more in keeping with a day in January than this one in June.

The route from Beinn Fhionnlaidh to our next peak, which we named Ben Chrysanthemum in the absence of a Gaelic speaker to keep us right, took us along a vibrant green glen to a hanging valley with a corrie and lochan that offered a perfect camping spot, lush and still. Mental note was made to return one day. It was tempting to linger and savour the solitude, but we reminded ourselves that this running business was a serious endeavour and Rabbie and his electronic tracker could not wait for dawdling picnickers.

Kirsty Maguire enjoying a nice cuppa in from of the stove in Alltbeithe Youth Hostel. Photo: Katherine Lawlor

We had chosen the north-east ridge for our summit approach rather than the east ridge due to lengthy speculation about avalanche risk and slope aspects. As the ground steepened we needed to wield the ice axes we had brought along 'just in case', making our way up some very steep ground, the usually rocky ridge shored up with snow, just like the Hillary Step on Everest. The summit of our Everest afforded us spectacular views and satisfied grins for the photos. Welcome sunshine banished the last of the mountain demons.

Once at the top we could see that the eastern ridge that we had so carefully avoided was almost snow free and we skipped lightly down this one waving our axes with happy abandon. Once the ground on the ridge flattened out there followed a significant post-summit slump in energy, requiring consumption of a large number of jelly babies. On the resulting sugar high we made fast progress off the hill towards the remote Alltbeithe Hostel, happily removing layers of fleece and waterproofs as an unfamiliar sun beat down, broiling us in our plastic wrappers. We found Paul Fettes, looking slightly anxious, peering out of the youth hostel window. Rabbie was passed on to the next pair of fresh running legs (my partner for my previous leg, Nick Leslie, and Gary Mooney on his first outing in the Challenge) and we sat down to a fine cup of rehydrating tea in the rather bohemian surroundings of one of the most remote hostels in Britain.

Behind the Scenes of the Archie Challenge
(with apologies to David Attenborough)
By Paul Fettes and Ben Ulyatt

Paul: While Elspeth and I were having our arctic adventure on the Carn Eighe horseshoe, (and Nick and Kirsty were driving round to Glen Affric), Ben was driving north to join us in the Archie van – a rather aptly named VW Transporter which was provided for the Challenge by the John Clark Motor Group. It had been used to transport a whole pile of kit from Dundee for the first weekend, and back there afterwards. From now it was to become invaluable as a transporter of kit and people for the Challenge itself.

Ben: The day started simply enough for me, at home with typical logistic and transition duties for the AMC. I set off early for the four-hour drive up to Glen Affric in our sponsored Archie van, carrying bikes, camping gear, winter mountaineering kit, and perhaps most importantly home baking supplies for the troops. With poor mobile reception, communications were somewhere between intermittent and non-existent, but Paul and I met in the Glen Affric car park exactly as planned.

Paul: Now any self-respecting nature programme has plenty of behind the scenes to-ing and fro-ing, and so it was with the Challenge. As the BBC has discovered, it makes sense to give it a mention. We were called upon for a little such action the next day. It would make life a lot easier for Katherine and Kirsty if they could cycle alongside Loch Affric, and up the glen to the point where they would dump the bikes and start their run towards Beinn Fhionnlaidh. Equally once they finished at Alltbeithe Hostel it would be good for them to be able to ride out. By the same token, the next set of runners could save their legs if they pedalled gently up to Alltbeithe before their run from the hostel over to Kintail. Unfortunately, we quickly realised that didn't add up. It meant four bikes going in but only two people coming out, unless somebody else could collect two bikes. We would not be carrying Rabbie, and tracker watchers back home would be oblivious to our endeavours, but they would be important for the smooth running of the Challenge.

Great! So after a large breakfast, Ben and I jogged along the 12 or so kilometres to the point where the girls had left their bikes. We rode them up to Alltbeithe Hostel where

Paul heading up Glen Affric on foot and on bike. Photos: Ben Ulyatt

we met up with Nick and Gary who cycled the whole way in. We had a bit of a wait, which was made substantially more pleasant by a cup of tea and some cake, sitting by a warm stove in the cosy hostel. We were starting to get a little bit worried by the time Katherine and Kirsty finally arrived looking tired and rosy-cheeked from their endeavours. Despite the prospect of heading up three fairly ominous looking jagged peaks in the late afternoon, Messrs Leslie and Mooney looked remarkably enthusiastic as they embarked on what we expected to be the last leg of the day.

Ben: As he set off on the next leg Gary asked, 'Can you take my sweaty bib shorts back?' 'It's OK, I'll wear them,' I replied. This questionable decision was compensated by the cycle back again on Gary's carbon mountain bike which was very comfy... or perhaps it was the shorts.

Paul: We left Kirsty and Katherine at the hostel. They understandably seemed to be in no rush to leave, whereas we were keen to get going. Once we had cycled out (on Gary and Nick's bikes) we needed to drive the long way round to Kintail via the Great Glen, and if we got our skates on we might get there in time to catch dinner at the Cluanie Inn.

Thus we ran 12km and cycled 18km without carrying Rabbie.

Glen Affric to Kintail
By Gary Mooney – with Nick Leslie

I drove north with a feeling of excitement and mild trepidation: excitement because it was mid-week and I was off work for the next two days to play in the mountains; trepidation because of doubts about my body's ability to cope with two days in the mountains without breaking down. Passing through the Cairngorms, the sky was a benevolent blue, with fluffy white cotton-wool clouds. It was a far cry from the wintery weather experienced in the first few days of the Challenge. As a result of this weather, in addition to a mountain bike, my car was stuffed with all manner of summer and winter gear including an ice axe.

Arriving in Glen Affric I saw, amongst the vehicles, a van covered in Archie Challenge slogans and a motor home with bikes racked on the back. This confirmed objective one complete – I had made it to the right place. I already knew Paul and Ben, who left shortly after I arrived, but I was met by another rather energetic individual who introduced himself as Nick and offered his hand. 'Hasn't he just come out of the heather? I hope he has cleaned that hand,' I thought to myself. Having experienced the seclusion of my car journey and taken in the delights of the scenery on the way to Affric, meeting Nick offered a striking contrast. He was clearly caught up in the Archie bubble, and was excitedly talking at a hundred miles an hour. Our mission was to cycle in to Alltbeithe Youth Hostel, collect Rabbie from Katherine and Kirsty, and run south over three Archies to Loch Cluanie in Kintail. I packed as quickly as I could while Nick gave me a running commentary of events so far. Trying not to be rude, and although there seemed to be a degree of urgency to get going, I asked Nick to give me a moment just to make sure I had not forgotten anything.

We set off on mountain bikes and talked mountain bikes, which was an easy topic of conversation. I was happy to be cycling, about which I felt confident and competent, unlike my running which had been blighted by calf and achilles injuries for several years. Doubts about my body holding up resurfaced. During the ride Nick explained that Kirsty and Katherine (who would be handing over to us) had already been out on the hills for several hours, hence his urgency. He did not want to be late. He needn't have worried. Arriving at Alltbeithe Youth Hostel, we met up with familiar and friendly faces in the form of Paul and Ben. The hostel was warm and inviting, and we enjoyed lots of tea, cake and a good chat about the Challenge (and about the weather!) while we waited. Gradually we became a little concerned about the safety of the girls out on the hill, but they duly arrived safely, tired but exhilarated by their adventure. Everyone was extremely pleased and a little relieved to see them. As we were about to leave, Paul stressed to us the priority of safety over that of proceeding at all costs. He wanted us to get down safely whether or not we reached our intended Archie summits.

Leaving the warm confines of the hostel, Nick and I crossed the soggy, boggy glen floor and made a beeline for our first obstacle, a deer fence. We scrambled over this and headed straight up the hill. Thankfully my calf seemed to be holding up OK. I had been over these hills from Cluanie before, but never from the Affric side. Knowing we had favourable daylight and good wind direction with regard to possible windslab developing, I thought the only difficulty might be the narrow ridge between our first Archie, Mullach Fraoch-choire (1102m), and our second one, A'Chralaig (1120m). We gained height quickly and, following deer tracks, headed west, chatting as we went. As we approached the top the wind speed increased but the gradient became a little more forgiving, which allowed us to ease back into a run. We arrived on a very windy summit, posed for a quick photo with Rabbie, and headed south at quite a lick.

When we arrived at the ridge we realised how cautious we would have to be. It was very steep, covered with snow, and there was quite a gale blowing. Despite this we crossed with relative ease, having to change our route just the once. So far the weather gods had been kind to us, but as we headed toward A'Chralaig, the cloud rolled in and it looked threatening. It cleared as we hit the summit – another quick photo and we were off again, this time at a good run. Again the cloud rolled in. Having followed our noses, and not having been forced to navigate, we were suddenly aware of not really knowing how far down the ridge we were. We had checked the map on the summit, and were aware that although we should initially follow the ridge south, we had to turn eastwards off it towards the Bealach Choire a'Chait. A wee window in the cloud revealed a peak. Ah, could this be the way? We turned east off the ridge and dropped on to a slope covered with snow. Nick stopped asking if he should have his ice axe out. It was only at this point that I realised where it was. It was placed upside down on the back of his bag with the shaft spike aimed directly at the base of his skull! I asked him to remove it from there, pointing out that

Nick Leslie on the way to Kintail. Photo: Gary Mooney

if he slipped he could impale himself on the shaft. While Nick rearranged himself I looked at the direction of slope and decided that we were going the wrong way, and that the peak we had seen in the cloud break was not the one we wanted. This was becoming a comedy of errors. We changed direction and headed across the snow slope onto some fairly level ground and into the bealach. There the cloud lifted again, and in front of us was the ridge up to Sgurr nan Conbhairean (1109m). We ascended the ridge to the summit as quickly as possible. One brief photo stop later, we descended to the roadside on the shore of Loch Cluanie, just as the light was fading. There we met a very happy looking Paul, who told us that we had made such good progress that he thought the two Cluanie hills could be done tonight. With that he took Rabbie and set off for a short ride to the Cluanie Inn, red tail-light blinking in the dusk. A few minutes later, Nick and I made our way to the same destination where we met Andy Forrester and Colin Donald. As we enjoyed a last-minute beer and venison casserole, Ben and Paul were already heading up into the dark mountains.

The Cluanie Inn
By Colin Donald – with Andrew Forrester

We had heard the reports of extreme winter conditions, and being fair-weather hill walkers with limited winter skills, Andrew and I travelled north with a mixed sense of apprehension and excitement. With only a very vague idea of where Rabbie was due to a poor phone signal and complete lack of internet, we relied on meeting the team in Glen Shiel. The Cluanie Inn looked like a good option for a rendezvous point, so we pitched the tent within walking distance. It seemed unlikely that we would be doing anything until the following morning, and the decision was therefore made to kick back for the evening. Venison casserole was duly ordered and washed down with a couple of fine local ales. Paul and Ben finally managed to get in touch. After a busy day running in and cycling out from the youth hostel in Glen Affric, they were making the long road trip round in the Archie camper van and the Archie Transporter. We put in a request for a couple of late meals from the kitchen so that they weren't left hungry.

Around 9pm they arrived looking exhilarated, and buzzing from the day's activity. I was now very comfortable in the warmth of the pub and contemplating my third pint of ale; Paul put a little dampener on things by saying, 'I wouldn't have too much beer, it'll be an early start. I was hoping you guys could get going at 4am.' I honestly thought he was joking, but Andrew replied, 'I wondered if you might say that.' As we expected, the plan was for us to run over the two Archies next to the Inn, but I had not expected quite such an early start. However, the fluid nature of this challenge was demonstrated shortly after, when Paul received a call from Nick, who reported better-than-expected progress out on the hill. 'Gary and Nick are on the way down from their last mountain. I'll head along to meet them and cycle back. Ben, I think we could do these two tonight. Will you be ready?' He wolfed down the rest of his food and was gone.

I realised a few minutes later that he was not joking. Shortly after 10pm, in fading light, we headed outside to find Paul and Ben kitting up for a stealth/night mission up Aonach Meadhoin and Sgurr a'Bhealaich Dheirg. We were now to do the next section, over three of the Five Sisters of Kintail: Sgurr na Ciste Duibhe, Sgurr na Carnach, and Sgurr Fhuaran. 'Oh, and can you be ready to start at 03:30?' We watched in disbelief as Paul and Ben started up towards a snow- and ice-encrusted ridge in the dark. We headed back to the tent, feeling rather stunned, and I didn't sleep a wink worrying about Paul and Ben, and wintery conditions on the north Shiel Ridge.

Gary Tompsett
June 3, 2015

Watchin' that tracker... Will the team attempt a night-time raid on those two Cluanie ARCHIEs I wonder??

👍 6

👍 Like   ➢ Share

Gary Tompsett's prophetic post number one

Cluanie Duo
By Ben Ulyatt with Paul Fettes

'Ben, can you be ready in half an hour to go up the two Cluanie hills in the dark?' Paul asked. Who could say no to someone so enthusiastic, who by his own admission was having difficulty planning and prioritising, whilst recovering from a significant head injury?

So at 10pm we set off into the dark up Aonach Meadhoin (1001m). A slog over the boggy moor warmed us up for a climb through knee deep snow fields, grass and heather, and up over rock to the first peak. Keen to make the most of the last remnants of daylight, we descended at pace over firm ground to the col. From there it was on with the head torches for the climb up number two, Sgurr a'Bhealaich Dheirg (1036m).

Prior to the Challenge, I had run over a few hills in training for a mountain marathon. I had absolutely no mountaineering experience. The last few metres could therefore be described as a bit of a 'baptism of ice' as I followed Paul along a precarious snow clad arête, in the dark, ignoring the 100m drop to our right. 'Fun and exhilarating' would be an understatement!

Midnight passed as we retraced our steps, first gingerly, then more quickly as the ground became less precipitous. From just above the col we turned due south off the ridge, and got our route down the shoulder of the hill just about right as we descended at speed over steep grass and heather moor. As we ran out from under the clag hugging the ridge we were greeted by the most wonderful moonrise in the east. Below us we could see the lights of the camper on the road in Glen Shiel, which made navigation easy as we picked our way through scruffy pine-forest remnants for the last part of our adventure. We arrived at the van at 1am wide awake and ready for more adventures the next day.

DAY 6
4 June 2015
7 ARCHIES

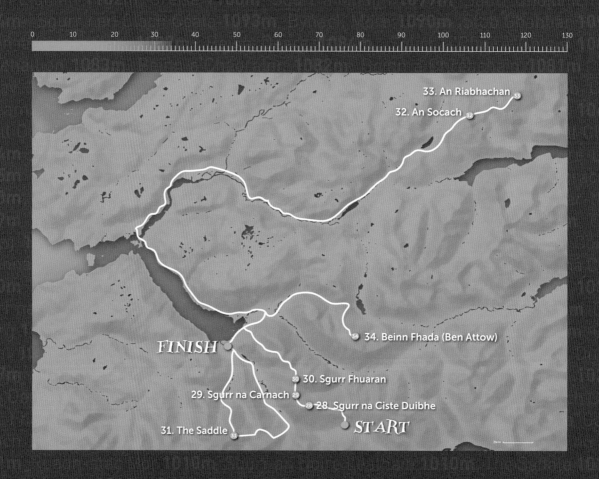

33. An Riabhachan

32. An Socach

34. Beinn Fhada (Ben Attow)

FINISH

30. Sgurr Fhuaran

29. Sgurr na Carnach

28. Sgurr na Ciste Duibhe

31. The Saddle

START

KINTAIL SISTERS

28. Sgurr na Ciste Duibhe (1027m), 29. Sgurr na Carnach (1002m), 30. Sgurr Fhuaran (1067m): Colin Donald & Andrew Forrester. 10km (1280m)

ROAD CYCLE LINK

Ben Ulyatt. 6km (80m)

THE SADDLE

31. The Saddle (1010m): Nick Leslie & Gary Mooney. 11km (1080m)

CYCLE LINK

Kirsty Maguire. 23km (400m)

THIRD TIME LUCKY

2. An Socach (1069m), 33. An Riabhachan (1129m): Ben Ulyatt & Paul Fettes. 26km cycle (204m) and 24km run (1460m)

ROAD CYCLE LINK

Peter Ross. 21km (360m)

BEINN FHADA (BEN ATTOW)

34. Beinn Fhada (Ben Attow, 1032m): Giles Ruck & Russell Duncan. 16km (1080m)

ROAD CYCLE RETURN

Russell Duncan. 5km (50m)

*Distance in kilometres, (and ascent in metres – this is the cumulative ascent of the leg, even if there is a net descent and the finish is lower than the start). In some cases there was a walk (or run) in or out to the start or finish of a leg without carrying the baton.

An early morning with the Sisters of Kintail
By Colin Donald – with Andrew Forrester

The alarm went at 3am and we awoke on a clear and perfectly still morning to find the tent surrounded by deer. After a short drive we met the others in Glen Shiel at our starting point for the ridge, and were relieved to find Paul and Ben in one piece after an epic night in the hills. It seemed that we had scored the first decent bit of weather the Challenge had seen and, adrenalised, we headed straight up the steep initial ascent to the start of the ridge. After a fairly rapid, thigh-burning ascent we made it onto the ridge path and were met with an incredible sunrise, and the sun continued to warm our backs as we started trotting west on an icy footpath in spectacular scenery.

After the anxieties of the last 24 hours it turned out to be one of my most enjoyable days in the hills, with only a few minor tumbles as we descended 'off-piste' to Shiel Bridge. I could not believe it was only 8am! After a short cycle link, Rabbie was duly passed on to Gary Mooney and Nick Leslie, the true mountain men of the previous day, and it was off to Forcan Ridge and The Saddle.

Andrew Forrester on the North Shiel ridge. Photo: Colin Donald

Saddle sore
By Gary Mooney – with Nick Leslie

The good news for me was that my body had held up; well, apart from two massive and painful heel blisters. The Saddle (1010m) is an iconic point in Glen Shiel. Its narrow East Ridge of Sgurr nan Forcan provides a superb and exposed scramble, with the crux being a tricky descent onto the summit slopes. The last time I had been on this mountain I turned around after wading through thigh-deep snow in the winter of 1998 while trying to get to the Forcan Ridge. Now, in summer, June 4th 2015, there was snow on the ground again, only this time not as much. I taped up my heels as well as I could, before Nick and I made our way along the A87 to the stalkers' path where the route begins. There we waited for Ben, who was cycling towards us to hand over. Once in possession of Rabbie, we were off.

Every step was painful as we moved quickly up the very well-constructed stalkers' path to the col at Biod an Fhithich, then ascended towards the Forcan Ridge. I was so glad to start climbing and relieve the pain from my heels. It was apparent that the Compeed and tape had moved. Nick was going very well and helped enormously by chatting away to me. We discovered a common work theme around cancer, albeit from different ends of the cancer spectrum. He ran a cancer research lab, whereas I worked directly with patients, treating those recently diagnosed with cancer and other people who had had treatment.

The weather had most definitely changed from earlier in the week. We had excellent visibility and thought ourselves to be very lucky. We climbed the exposed ridge, which was mostly free of snow, and descended the difficult step. At the summit we took the obligatory selfie, and traversed a steep corrie head wall to get onto the north ridge that would lead us back to Shiel Bridge campsite.

Descending the ridge was easy and delightful. We saw a fox and several mountain hare, and savoured stunning views of Skye. Moreover, I was not feeling any pain from blisters. However, things got trickier once we hit Sgurr na Creige and started descending through the bands of crags and buttresses that wrap around the ridge. We picked our way carefully on the descent, which was more difficult than the Forcan ridge. We went down some really steep gullies on loose shale type slopes,

Beer 'n' blisters. Photo: Gary Mooney

past a rather aromatic dead sheep. This obstacle seemed to go on and on. One slope of loose ground followed another. It was the type of terrain where deer escape to, and humans marvel at how they got there! Our progress slowed, as we had to be very precise where we placed a foot, hoping that whoever was above did not slip and fall onto whoever was below!

Finally, after what seemed like an age, we came through onto less demanding ground. Nick set off at a canter, encouraging me to follow. I did reluctantly, and as is usually the case, the pain from the blisters melted into the kind of background pain that you know is there, it's just not screaming. It leaves that for later. Once we hit the glen footpath Nick picked up the pace and we ran into the campsite, handing Rabbie over to cyclist Kirsty Maguire, and were greeted by well-wishers and more fresh Archie warriors ready to challenge themselves.

My blisters were sore for a further three weeks. For the first week I could not wear shoes but made do with flip-flop style footwear. I would like to thank Pete Ross for the kind donation of some dressings which helped enormously. Despite the blisters, my body held up and gave me hope that I may get running again. Furthermore, the blisters were easily worth being part of such a mammoth endeavour as the Archie Challenge. Thanks also to Paul Fettes. You have great vision and a sound social conscience.

Third time lucky:
The Two Elusive Archies An Socach and An Riabhachan,
By Ben Ulyatt – with Paul Fettes

This was the third attempt at the two elusive Archies: An Socach (1069m) and An Riabhachan (1129m). Previous attempts from the leeward east were hampered by deep snow, cornices, gales and blizzards. But our attempt was from the windward west, which would hopefully, theoretically and alliteratively, work wonders.

Despite it being June, as someone with zero winter mountaineering experience, the morning started with a lesson from Paul on what to do with an ice axe when you are falling off a mountain...

While Kirsty cycled round from Shiel Bridge, we enjoyed a spectacular and scenic drive to meet her. We passed the iconic Eilean Donan castle, shortly after which we turned off the main road to Skye, and instead followed a little, undulating B-road for a short distance to a wee car park at the head of the inappropriately named but beautiful Loch Long. Neither of us had been here before, and the exploration of little corners of our country were one of the unexpected pleasures of the Challenge.

Once Kirsty arrived, we set off from the car park on our cyclo-cross bikes. We immediately passed through the delightful hamlet of Killilan before making our way up a farm track to the Iron Lodge. Laden with full winter running gear we rapidly overheated, but enjoyed the 13km uphill ride with some of the best weather to date during the Challenge. We ditched the bikes, swapping bike shoes and helmets for trail shoes and Buffs, and set off on foot up the ominously named Coffin Road.

The pace started high along well-trodden paths, and we soon drenched our feet through the many overflowing streams. As we approached Loch Mhoicean and headed north-east up to and along the ridge to An Socach, the terrain turned to moorland and bog, which slowed our progress to, at times, a literal crawl. As the weather closed in and temperature dropped, the terrain improved and we were surprised at how straightforward our progress had been. In minimal visibility we found the trig point for the obligatory selfie with Rabbie and put all our kit on to ward off the cold.

Ben Ulyatt on An Socach, looking towards An Riabhachan. Photo: Paul Fettes

Then the cloud parted for a brief spell, opening up superb views to the north and west over Loch Monar and the Archies beyond. This also revealed the problems to the east and south encountered by the previous attempts: deep snow down steep ridges, with huge cornices and precipitous drops. No shame in not getting up that in gales and whiteout!

Our next aim was An Riabhachan which lay four kilometres to the north-east along a steep rocky ridge, with paths and footprints visible in the snow. Running at pace down massive snow fields to the col was exhilarating, though we knew it meant that ascent would follow. Our route for the final few kilometres was straightforward, and after picking our way up the ridge we made good progress along hard snow and frozen ground to the top.

Having reached the summit of An Riabhachan, and with the great satisfaction of bagging these two elusive Archies, we turned back the way we came for the 12km back to the bikes. Ironically this meant going back over An Socach for a second time, proving that mountain summits can sometimes be like buses! On the descent we encountered a poor roe deer, sheltered but dying in a ravine in the moor. There was nothing we could do and so, sadly, we continued running, now at reasonable speed back down past the loch.

The bike back down the farm tracks started at speed on our knobbly tyres, but was soon slowed first by a puncture, and then by Highland cows who insisted on sauntering along the middle of the track leaving no room to pass! We finally arrived back at the rendezvous in Killilan at 9pm, tired but happy. Not a bad way to spend seven hours!

A crash and a bike ride
By Pete Ross

I arrived at base camp in the Shiel Bridge campsite in the late afternoon. Not knowing what to expect, I was greeted with a bowl of pasta (a recurring theme during my brief participation), and immediately felt at ease. My instructions were to prepare to do the short evening cycle transfer from one glen to the next, receiving Rabbie from Paul and Ben, and passing him on to Russell Duncan and Giles Ruck, who had a late evening run up Beinn Fhada (Ben Attow).

Nick drove me in Paul's aunt's camper van to meet Ben and Paul, transporting my bike on the back. As we entered the estate where we were to meet, Paul came flying down the track on his bike. Great! Nick, busy discussing the challenges of reversing the camper van, was obviously delighted, selected reverse and... CRUNCH! Uh oh. Paul's face told it all. Shock and dismay rolled into one. While worried about the van, my bike that was going to transport Rabbie was also directly in the impact zone, so I walked round the van with trepidation. The bike was fine. The van, well let's just say there were some structural changes to the rear bumper!

The ride to the drop off was not long. It was just after 9pm, roads quiet, smooth rolling tarmac, 13½ miles, height gain 45m, taking 45 minutes. It was still and moody, but a cracking wee ride along the side of Lochs Long and Duich. Russell and Giles looked keen at the handover – I was envious of the challenge they had ahead...

Gary Tompsett's prophetic post number two

Beinn Fhada (or is it Attow?)
By Russell Duncan – with Giles Ruck

Those Archie Mountain Challenge boys and girls had been having a hard time of it. Snow, ice, large volumes of meltwater (rivers in spate) and generally very unseasonable conditions had been making life difficult. The team looked like they could do with a hand, and back home some of us were feeling left out of the action. OK. So, what to do about it?

- Late night on-call shift at work in Dundee, ✅
- Invigilate postgraduate exam in Edinburgh in the morning, ✅
- Drive from Edinburgh to Shiel Bridge Campsite, ✅.
- Meet some crazies in a motor home, ✅
- Wait for some other nut cases to get off the hill after deciding to take two previously unapproachable Archies from the rear, ✅
- Run up Beinn Fhada (or is it Attow?) with Giles Ruck, starting at 10pm, ✅
- Run back down and then cycle from Morvich back to Shiel Bridge Campsite, ✅
- Sleep in back of a Ford S-Max for two hours, ✅
- Get up and cycle part of the way up Glen Shiel, surrounded by hundreds of red deer grazing at the side of the road in the dawn glory, ✅
- Hand Rabbie over to two more crazies, ✅
- Drive back to Dundee, rest, recharge, smile, and get ready for more of the same next week, ✅

Beinn Fhada with Giles Ruck was Type 2 fun at its best! I had been informed by a friend and fellow mountain enthusiast that the stalkers' path was runnable, and they were so right. From the off Giles and I were keen to enjoy our night-time jaunt, while trying to make it as brief as possible. The terrain and weather allowed this to be achieved, and Giles' navigation was spot on. This was my first experience of nocturnal hill running and I enjoyed every minute of it!

Andrew Forrester on the North Glen Shiel ridge. Photo: Colin Donald

DAY 7
5 June 2015
6 ARCHIES

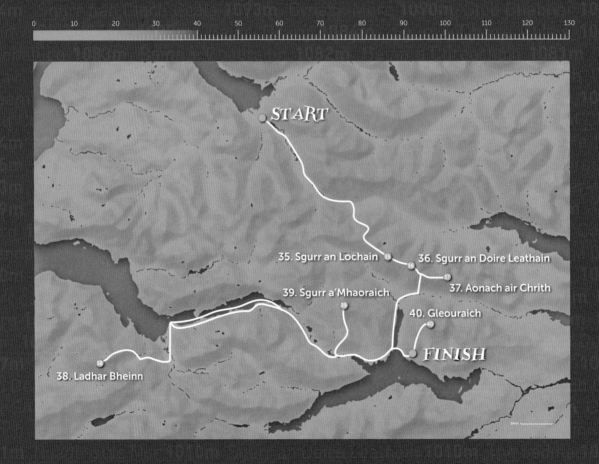

START

35. Sgurr an Lochain

36. Sgurr an Doire Leathain

37. Aonach air Chrith

39. Sgurr a'Mhaoraich

40. Gleouraich

FINISH

38. Ladhar Bheinn

ROAD CYCLE

Shiel Bridge to hill start: Russell Duncan 9km (220m)

SOUTH SHIEL RIDGE

35. Sgurr an Lochain (1004m), 36. Sgurr an Doire Leathain (1010m), 37. Aonach air Chrith (1021m): Pete Ross & Matthew Bull. 15km (1540m), run out 3km.

CYCLO-CROSS / ROAD CYCLE LINK

to Kinloch Hourn: Dave Henderson. 13km (170m)

LADHAR BEINN

38. Ladhar Bheinn (1020m): Kirsty Maguire & Giles Ruck. 25km (1670m), 9km walk out.

SEA KAYAK

from Barisdale to Kinloch Hourn – David Henderson, Richard & Fiona Maguire. 11km.

ROAD CYCLE LINK

Kinloch Hourn to Sgurr a'Mhaoraich start: Paul Fettes. 5km (270m)

SGURR A'MHAORAICH

39. Sgurr a'Mhaoraich (1027m): Paul Fettes. 7km (790m)

ROAD CYCLE LINK

to Gleouraich start: Craig Cumming & Jason Hardy. 7km (120m)

GLEOURIACH

40. Gleouraich (1035m): Craig Cumming & Jason Hardy 7km (840m)

*Distance in kilometres, (and ascent in metres – this is the cumulative ascent of the leg, even if there is a net descent and the finish is lower than the start). In some cases there was a walk (or run) in or out to the start or finish of a leg without carrying the baton.

An early awakening for the South Shiel Ridge
By Pete Ross and Matthew Bull

Pete: Knock, knock. Russell's face appeared at my car window, at 3:40am... Ugh. Russell had wanted to check I was up before heading off with Rabbie. Thanks! The plan was to meet Rabbie at the chosen entry point to the South Shiel Ridge at 04:30, and I had hoped for another 20 minutes sleep. The schedule had been decided at the team meeting the night before. This was a thing of marvel – six folk, all 'soloists' by day in their chosen professions, working as a well-oiled machine with a shared goal. Mathew Bull and I were grouped together as the 'fresh meat' for this leg. A long run with three Archies on the South Shiel ridge. It was suggested that we should miss out the first third of the ridge as it had no Archies, and use a path that went up from the road a little farther up Glen Shiel. It sounded good, and should make it shorter.

Matthew: My initial attempt at getting involved in the Archie Challenge at Achnasheen was unfortunately curtailed in fairly spectacular fashion by Norovirus, which was unwittingly imported from New Zealand by my one-year-old nephew. Having spent many evenings planning an entire section of the Challenge, not to be able to make it into the mountains was a huge disappointment. Fortunately, the Challenge was longer than your average ultra-marathon, so I finally had the chance to join the action in Kintail.

Pete: After the painfully early rise, Matthew and I were handed a cuddly baton by Russell at the prearranged meeting point, and we wished him well he set off back to work in Dundee! We found the path and set off. Unfortunately it only lasted about 300m before disappearing into a new deer fence. Over the fence there was nothing to follow, and all we could do was go straight up the side of the ridge. It was slow, and not the run we had planned. We were under a bit of time pressure, because the weather forecast wasn't great, and because we did not want to further delay the rabbit on its journey. The first two miles took an hour, gaining 780m.

Matthew: We set off on an overcast but dry day. It was great to accompany Rabbie into the hills, and he was placed on the outside of the rucksack so he could get great views of the route that we were taking. Despite Pete being more accustomed to being on two wheels than two feet, keeping up with him was a challenge in itself as we wound our way up onto the ridge and over the relevant summits.

A rather bedraggled Rabbie savours the view on the South Glen Shiel ridge. Photo: Pete Ross

Pete: Once on the ridge, the view was breath-taking – high cloud allowed us to see peaks all around. We managed to pick up some pace, and picked off our first two peaks, Sgurr an Lochain (1004m) and Sgurr an Doire Leathain (1010m), in dry and bright conditions. Compulsory photos at the top of each provided our small part of the big jigsaw. The weather then turned, and the wind and sleet picked up. The last summit, Aonach Air Chrith (1021m), was the trickiest, with a fragile ridge, and I felt slightly more confident in the knowledge that Matthew works with the Mountain Rescue Team in Tayside. After the photo at the top, we raced back, took the zig zag stalkers' path down the south of the ridge and out to hand over.

Matthew: A quick three Archies later, a brief stop to video Rabbie on one of the tops, and we were on the way down to meet up with cyclist David Henderson. A well-travelled Archie rabbit was transferred to the bike and his journey continued on to Kinloch Hourn and Knoydart.

Pete: We were soaked and exhausted, but delighted to have been able to contribute. And it was only 10am! Fiona, Matthew's wife, was waiting in a warm car to drive us back to the start point. She also provided home baking which was a real life saver – hopefully the Challenge will also save lives in the long term.

Matthew: The Challenge wasn't just about the mountains, the planning or the fundraising. It became an addiction, tracking the live updates that allowed us all to see where the rabbit was at any one time. From a personal perspective the Challenge was fantastic to be involved in from beginning to end. I wish I could have done more days in the hills, but work and illness prevented that. In writing about the Challenge, I need to thank Dr Paul Fettes, without whom it would never have happened. It is great to have contributed in a small way to the creation of a new paediatric operating theatre suite for Dundee.

Cycle Link Glen Quoich to Kinloch Hourn
By David Henderson

Sleeping in a car is never the best and I was happy to be up early, even though there were some hungry midges about. From Shiel Bridge, I took the long drive round to Loch Quoich, parked by the northern finger of the loch that led towards the South Shiel Ridge. I had an easy cycle in on the west side of the loch in the rain, which became torrential as I waited for the Pete and Matthew in Glen Quoich near Alltbeithe House. No chance of a view up the hill as the clag was down to around 500m.

All of a sudden they appeared around a bend in the track, smiling and beaming! They looked pretty fresh considering they had been over three 1000-metre peaks in a cool three hours or so. Moments later I was off. Having never cycled the Kinloch Hourn road I enjoyed the swooping corners on the steep descent to Kinloch Hourn. Giles Ruck and Kirsty Maguire were waiting and eager to be on their way up Ladhar Bheinn in the Knoydart peninsula. This is a big hill rising from sea level to 1020m, over very challenging terrain in a very remote area. Just in case that outing wasn't enough, Giles had preceded it with a late night excursion up Beinn Fhada. You've got to hand it to these folk, no half measures!

I had driven up to Glen Shiel (where the team was based) the previous evening to find that there had been a change of plan. The initial plan of taking gear into Barisdale bothy and supporting at least two sets of runners with food and equipment for a big trip over the Knoydart hills (and out via Glen Dessarry to Loch Arkaig) had been shelved because the weather forecast was dire. The new plan was for Kirsty Maguire and Giles Ruck to run from Kinloch Hourn into Barisdale, up Ladhar Bheinn and back out the way they had come. The other hills would be picked off separately, in more bite-sized chunks. I met Kirsty's parents, Richard and Fiona Maguire, in the comfort of their warm camper van. She had invited them along on the basis that they could get involved in the Challenge if there was a need for any sea kayaking. We agreed that such support on the way back from Barisdale would be helpful after what would be another big day for Giles and Kirsty.

At the road end in Kinloch Hourn, I watched the runners set off for their big day out, but after a few metres Kirsty about-turned and gave me the keys to her van. Ten minutes later I was glad she had, as the rain was bouncing off the roof of the van, the road and the loch. Knoydart was definitely living up to its reputation as the wettest place in Scotland.

From Knoydart, via New Zealand to the Himalaya: Ladhar Bheinn, the most westerly Archie
By Kirsty Maguire – with Giles Ruck

Our run started off well but quickly deteriorated. I was pretty tired after running and biking close to 200km in a week, and the coastal track into Barisdale is rough and undulating, so progress was slow. It was pelting down, it was soggy underfoot and there was not much visibility. This felt almost reassuringly familiar. We got as far as the bothy in Barisdale, and stopped for shelter and some food hoping the rain shower would pass. No such luck. Fortunately the bothy wasn't warm or we might have been more reluctant to leave. Heading over the beautiful bay and up the flanks of Ladhar Bheinn (1020m) was simply soggy. My mind wandered to west-coast New Zealand, re-living memories of wet tramping through stunning but barely visible landscape there too. We saw no one on the route in and, despite the rain, I found emptying my mind while putting one foot in front of the other as we climbed was curiously enjoyable.

Descending Ladhair Bheinn, with Barrisdale Bay and Loch Hourne in the background. Photo: Giles Ruck

We were enveloped by cloud as we gained height, and as we neared the summit I felt a strange sensation of being in a bubble. I felt shrouded from reality by the mist, and I could hardly see my hands in front of my face. Yet my other senses were heightened, and I was alert to sounds, and to changes in the feel of the terrain and the weather.

Following the path along the ridge was not too difficult, and at least there was no snow. As we approached the top we heard muffled voices and the ringing of a prayer bell. I was not sure whether I was being transported to the Alps with cowbells, or to the Himalaya with Nepali prayer flags and bells as we followed the sounds beckoning through the mists. Were we sailors about to meet a sticky end following the sound of mermaids singing? Instead we received a warm welcome from a lot of people on the summit with a prayer bell. Where on earth did they all appear from? We showed our delight in making it to the top by ringing the bell ourselves.

Heading away from the summit and quickly losing height, the clouds rolled back and the sun came out. We looked in awe at the seemingly endless mountains around us, the moody black sea and the track beside Loch Hourn along which we had come and were to return by. What a paradise. All the rain and dreams of travelling were immediately forgotten. We were back in the here and now, marvelling at everything around us. Certainly my brain was too tired to think much, and I was just drinking it all in. Giles filmed it for the benefit of the others. Admittedly running was fairly limited at this point, due to my weary limbs, but at least our way down was gravity assisted.

Despite the majestic surroundings, by the time we were nearing the bothy we were really keen to see those kayakers. With great anticipation we opened the door to the bothy... to find it completely empty. How disappointing. Managing not to sit down, we started walking along the track, trying to gather energy for the run out.

Walking towards us in this remote spot was a man in shorts, carrying a plastic shopping bag. We appraised the unusual choice of baggage before realising he was looking curiously at us as he ambled along. 'Are you the runners?' he asked (it was not really an apt description but there was no other sign of life and the Lycra may have been a give-away). 'There are sea kayakers up on the point waiting for you.' Oh happiness! Our pace picked right up and we trotted enthusiastically over to find them sunbathing in a beautiful cove. A rather bedraggled cloth rabbit was tucked up on the deck, Mum handed over some food to us and they paddled swiftly off towards a rainbow, with a following tide and the wind on their backs. Giles was so pleased that he did a wee dance. All I could do was sit in the sunshine, soak in the warmth and look forward to a leisurely walk back to Kinloch Hourn.

Rainbow on the Loch: Sea kayak
By Fiona Maguire and David Henderson
– with Richard Maguire

Fiona: Being retired, we have a bit less of an urge to stick to a plan in nasty weather, and it was very wet in Shiel Bridge when our daughter Kirsty left with Giles for their Knoydart run. It had been great to meet the ARCHIE team the night before, and we were captivated by the descriptions of angry mountains, the stamina of the runners, the elation on the summits, and the moments when the sun broke through. However, we felt less inspired in the morning rain. It was tempting to stay in our camper van, but we had agreed to join fellow kayaker David Henderson to ferry Rabbie back from Barisdale to Kinloch Hourn. We enjoyed spectacular views as we drove down to Kinloch Hourn, and manoeuvring round the picturesque bends seemed quite physical enough for one day. David was waiting for us by the side of the loch.

David: Kirsty's parents, Richard and Fiona, arrived with my car and their camper van after a few problems with starting engines. We had multiple cups of tea and cake to fortify us for the paddle down to Barisdale. Collectively we hoped if we delayed the start the rain might ease. Richard and I decided we'd better get organised as it would be an eight-kilometre paddle into the wind and through the narrows at Caolas Mor. We got wrapped up in our kayaking kit and set off. It wasn't long before we began to warm up. Our journey down the loch was eased by the good craic, fantastic light on the hills, and the stunning sea and mountain vista from what has been described as the most fjord-like loch in Scotland.

The sun appeared just as we arrived at Barrisdale Bay. The cloud zipped across the top of Ladhar Bheinn, the sun shone on the higher buttresses and Coire Dhorrcail didn't look so dark!

Fiona: Thankfully the rain was easing and there was no wind. We were early for the runners so we picnicked in ever improving weather. To pass the time we inspected heather leaves with a botanist's hand lens, and savoured other details that runners surely never see. Lo and behold, just when it was full hot sunshine, up popped two damp, weary-looking, but happy runners. Their job done, they handed Rabbie over to us, and were then able to set a more leisurely pace as they walked back out along the rough track back to Kinloch Hourn.

Kayakers in Barrisdale Bay. Photo: Kirsty Maguire

David: Giles and Kirsty uttered great whoops of joy when they appeared. They were clearly very happy about not having to run out along the coastal path. It was a really nice occasion to see Kirsty with her parents in such a remote place and share the 'Archie' experience with them.

Fiona: Wee Rabbie deserved a rest, and he got one. He was fastened to a kayak and basked in the sun, with a gentle following breeze and a following tide. He was able to savour a rainbow which appeared just as we came through the narrows, and then a double rainbow closer to home. By the time he reached Kinloch Hourn he was fully restored and ready to be snatched off on the next leg of his adventure.

Sgurr a'Mhaoraich
By Paul Fettes...
...and Gleouraich
By Craig Cumming and Jason Hardy

Craig: By the time I reached Loch Lochy I knew it was a good idea to come. There was a break in the weather and the sun was out, its rays making the water sparkle. The rain had filled the burns and waterfalls, making them cascade down the hillside. The road was quiet, and the trip was worth it for the drive alone, even in a camper van. I grew up in the West Highlands and hadn't been back since my parents sold up and moved to the east coast. I had forgotten quite how beautiful this part of the country is. It had been too long since I was last here.

When Paul suggested the Archie Mountain Challenge it sounded like an ambitious but crazy idea. Excellent, I thought. I like mountains; I'd like to be a part of that. I enlisted Jamie Smith and Neil Fettes who were daft enough to want to be part of it too. We're old kayaking friends from Uni who enjoyed some mountain biking before we had kids, and enjoy a stroll in the hills. But none of us are runners.

Paul quickly assembled a team of mountain runners and a cycling peloton and it soon became clear that we'd need to try to bring something different to the party if we were to be more useful than a parachute on a bicycle. Fortunately for us, the route required a couple of kayak legs. We booked a few days off at the time when we might be needed, and waited.

Celebrity Strictly Come Baking On Ice Factor became second rate viewing in our house for the weeks of the Challenge, and was replaced by 'Tracker Watch'. Where were the team now? What was the weather like? Had the team summitted? Why was the tracker stationary in the high mountains in bad weather when there was no bothy on the map? Who was going to get Barry's desk in our shared office if he really had frozen to death? There was enormous relief every time the tracker moved to a place of safety, or carried on its journey. Mobile phone reception was patchy, so communication was difficult and we were not sure when we might be needed. The tracker headed into Glen Garry.

View south from Sgurr a'Mhaoraich. In the distance is the ridge traversed the next day in stormy weather. Photo: Paul Fettes

'Sod it,' we said. 'We'll go anyway.' We'll bring food, beer, boats, bikes, maps, waterproofs, and a camper van complete with kitchen sink, and meet up by Kinloch Hourn. We'll probably be of no use to the Challenge apart from the food and beer and possibly the camper van but we'll go anyway. There is only one road in and out; we're bound to find them. I headed off the day before the other two, looking to catch the Archie team at some point late in the afternoon.

I found myself descending the steep, narrow, rocky single track road down to the car park at Kinloch Hourn in a seven-metre long, three-metre high and worryingly 2.3-metre wide camper van. Well, the snow plough and bin lorry presumably manage, and Paul's probably brought his aunt's van along here too, I thought...

Unfortunately I arrived too late, and found Dave Henderson packing up his sea kayak having finished relaying Rabbie out of Knoydart. Numbers were thinning, as many had had to return to work but the most westerly Archie – Ladhar Bheinn – had been reached and Rabbie was now back with Paul.

'Hi Craig, I'm off to cycle up the glen to the next mountain. Want to do an Archie?'

I agreed on the proviso that I had to eat first, and repeated I was no runner and didn't want to hold anyone back. We agreed that he would cycle to and then run up and down Sgurr a'Mhaoraich on his own in the daylight, as he could do this both quickly and safely.

Meanwhile Jason and I would shuttle a van and bikes to the right places so we could cycle on from the foot of Sgurr a'Mhaoraich to the foot of Gleouraich for a twilight climb.

Jason: After returning home for the week, I was eager to rejoin the crew for some more Archie action, so a quick drive up to Loch Quoich after work on Friday was in order. The road along to Kinloch Hourn is so quiet that it was a strange experience to come round a bend and find myself confronted by Paul Fettes on a bike! He was about to set off up Sgurr a'Mhaoraich on his own, breaking his two-person-per-leg rule. It was such a lovely evening, who could blame him? A brief chat to inform me I was climbing Gleouraich with Craig later, and he was off.

Paul: It is a steep rise out of Kinloch Hourn on hairpin bends, but I hardly noticed because the views from the road are spectacular and I relished drinking it all in as I pedalled upwards. Shortly after meeting Jason I got to the starting point of the run. I carried my bike off the road, left it behind a knoll and changed out of cycling footwear into my fell shoes. Sack back on and off we went. 'We' was pushing it a little as this was the only solo mountain leg of the entire Challenge. We had set the 'pairs on mountain legs' rule because it was safer. I took the executive decision to break it because the risks on this leg were pretty minimal. It was a short, out and back run. The weather conditions were fine, the visibility was excellent, and people knew the route I was taking.

I took a good track for a short way up towards some waterfalls on the Allt Coire Sgoireadail. Before I reached them, the track deteriorated, and it was time for me to head straight up the shoulder of Sgurr a'Mhaoraich (1027m), through steep tussocks of grass and heather, but the ground was firm and the vegetation thin enough that I found it fairly easy going. In what seemed like no time at all I was standing at the top with a large grin on face and only a rather grubby cloth rabbit for company, as I enjoyed a magnificent evening view over Knoydart and Kintail. Shafts of sunlight pierced through angry clouds and made the dancing waters of Loch Hourn glisten below me.

The descent was just plain fun. This was the best I had felt since the accident. I felt alert and very alive as I ran down the slope, enjoying the sort of exhilaration that is perhaps more normally experienced hurtling down a slope on a pair of skis, or on a mountain bike. As I descended I could see a van appear and stop on the side of the road. I got down to it to find a slightly flustered looking Jason and Craig.

Craig: Topography doesn't seem to affect Paul in the same way as most people. Normally, a cycle up a steep road from sea level, a yomp across a peat bog and a climb up and down a 1027m mountain would cause a person to break sweat, and take a period of some several hours, but no. As soon as Jay and I had finished the shuttle and taken the bikes off the rack, a sleek, fast moving creature appeared on the horizon like some kind of bipedal puma, and bounded down the hillside. The bog will slow him up, we agreed. It didn't.

Moments later Paul appeared, and we set off up the road on our bikes. At the bottom of Gleouraich (1035m) we quickly changed into hill walking kit... Wait a minute, why was Jason getting changed into what looked suspiciously like running kit? The answer became quickly apparent as the quality of the light started to fade and the Scottish drizzle thickened up into a light rain. As we jogged gently up along a good quality path that became progressively steeper the higher we got, Jason suggested, 'Fancy running for a bit?' I thought I was already, but I picked up the pace a little, and we found the sweet spot where Jason managed to avoid hypothermia and I managed to avoid cardiac arrest.

Jason: A well-built path takes you up the south-east shoulder and we made good time. At one point we could see the lights of the Archie camper van convoy snaking their way back up the glen from Kinloch Hourn.

Craig: We arrived at the summit after the wind picked up but just before darkness fell. We posed for a picture, paused briefly to allow our phones to connect with the outside world with the mountains out of the way, and then plunged into the darkness with head torches on. We descended with a welcome headwind which softened the blow every time our feet struck the ground, taking the strain off our knees. In fairness, Jason probably didn't notice, but this old kayaker's knees were very grateful.

Jason: It was back down to the waiting camper vans for curry and beer. Finish work on Friday and bag an Archie before bedtime. Is there a better way to end the working week?

DAY 8
6 June 2015
3 ARCHIES

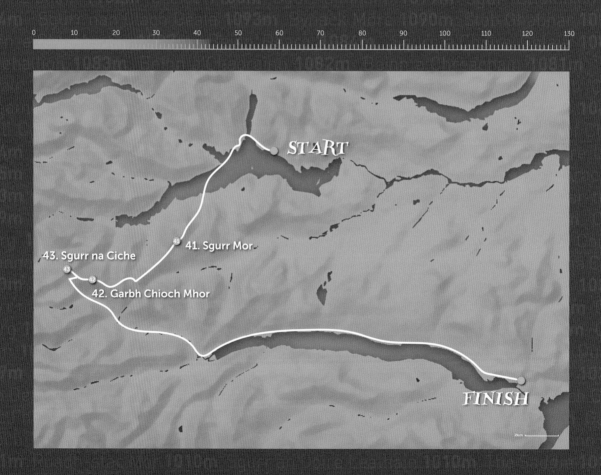

START

41. Sgurr Mor

43. Sgurr na Ciche

42. Garbh Chioch Mhor

FINISH

2km

SHORT ROAD CYCLE

Cycle to Loch Quoich: Kirsty Maguire. 4km (50m)

LOCH QUOICH PADDLE

Paul Fettes, Jason Hardy, Jamie Smith & Craig Cumming. 3km

LOCH QUOICH TO GLEN DESSARRY

41. Sgurr Mor (1003m), 42. Garbh Chioch Mhor (1013m), 43. Sgurr na Ciche (1040m): Paul Fettes & Jason Hardy. 20km (1710m), 4km run out.

MOUNTAIN/ROAD CYCLE

Glen Dessarry to Loch Arkaig outlet: Jamie Smith & Neil Fettes. 25km (400m)

---

*Distance in kilometres, (and ascent in metres – this is the cumulative ascent of the leg, even if there is a net descent and the finish is lower than the start). In some cases there was a walk (or run) in or out to the start or finish of a leg without carrying the baton.

Stormy crossing, stormy ridge

By Jason Hardy, Craig Cumming, Paul Fettes with Jamie Smith

Jason: Over curry and beers the previous night, Paul, Craig and I had discussed the plan for the next day. The Knoydart runners and kayakers were to head away, which would leave just the three of us. Craig had a couple of kayaking friends coming to join us, one of whom was due to pitch up first thing in the morning. Another runner (John Irving) was also due to arrive at some point, but we weren't sure when, or if he was bringing anyone else with him. It almost goes without saying that we had no phone signal to contact anyone.

Craig: We spent quite a while debating the thorny issue of how to get to the hills to the south of Loch Quoich without going for many miles around it, and without having to cross rivers in spate in the process. The forecast was for rain and hurricane-force winds, and many had assumed that this would be a rest day for Rabbie as the storm blew through. The cycle round to Loch Arkaig was very long, and would leave a massive run. Ideally we should get to the south shore of Loch Quoich, but the run round the shore of the loch was barred by rivers that were likely to be impassable.

Jason: Having done it before, I suggested that canoeing across the loch would save time. We still had two sea kayaks, Craig had his kayak, and his friend was arriving with one in the morning. It goes without saying that when I suggested it, I was not anticipating doing it!

Craig: Jason suggested paddling across. I suspect this was safe in the knowledge that no one would be daft enough to agree. Paul immediately agreed.

Kirsty's parents offered to stick around, and to lend us their beautiful sea kayaks and split paddles for the crossing. A sea kayak is the perfect boat to cross a choppy loch in. Jamie was due to arrive in the morning and we would accompany the runners across the loch, and tow their boats back. We could then relocate to Loch Arkaig and wait there for them at the end of their run.

'That was a bit choppy.' Craig Cumming, Jamie Smith and Paul Fettes on the south shore of Loch Quoich. Photo: Jason Hardy

Paul: Jason's suggestion to kayak across the loch made eminent sense, except for the hostile weather conditions. The other side of Loch Quoich was a tantalising three kilometres kayak away, in comparison to a slow undulating 80km cycle round. The 'run round the loch' option did not look great either. Although the loch looked choppy, it was not a sea loch, so surely the waves couldn't be that big. Hopefully we would get some shelter from the hills that nestled the west end of the loch. Although I was, by the sound of it, the least experienced paddler, I had done a wee bit before. The thought of the trip filled me with dread, but it seemed like the best option. The deciding factor for me was the kind Maguire offer of use of their dry-suits as well as their boats.

Jason: Morning came, and with it strong winds and rain. Paul was excited at the paddling option. I was just praying John would arrive and that he and Paul could embark on this escapade. As we organised kit it became evident that John was not going to be there in time and I resigned myself to doing the leg with Paul. I had no-one to blame but myself for suggesting it in the first place.

Kit was donned, boats were launched and the usual logistics of moving cars and handover points were organised. I had Kirsty's Mum's sea kayak which was a little

Jamie and Craig return having deposited Paul and Jason. Photo: Kirsty Maguire

snug but I just managed to shoehorn myself in. The dry-suits were certainly reassuring given the conditions. The four of us set out, and as we poked our noses out of the bay into the loch the strength of the wind and swell became evident. It was enough to send me scurrying over to a fisherman camped nearby with a boat, to ask for a lift. He was not prepared to go out on the loch that day! Only one thing for it, then...

Craig: Paul and Jason took the sea boats, which were excellent but not their own, so not fitted out for maximum stability and comfort. Jamie and I took our white water play boats which are stable, comfortable and perfectly fitted but relatively slow in the water. My boat especially has the aerodynamics of a brick. Our landing point was on the southern shore, a mile or so to the west and into the headwind. The plan was that we would paddle up the shoreline until we were level with the egress then cross. Jamie and I were to shepherd the 'weaker' paddlers across and tow the boats back.

Half way up the shoreline we came out of the lee of a small hill and it became apparent to Jason that speed made for stability, and stability was in shorter supply than anticipated. He charged across the loch, with Paul and Jamie following along behind. I lagged behind in my 'brick' and decided to use the wind to ferry glide across the loch, and into the lee of the hills to the south.

Jason: As we got farther out into the loch it became choppier. I was squeezed into a boat too small for me, my hips were wedged and my knees jammed against the side. I knew that if I went over I was going to struggle to get out. The only thing for it was to keep the kayak nose into the wind and focus on the far side. Turning round and getting side-on to the swell and the wind was not an option. Beyond midway the swell became less as we gained shelter from the hills.

Paul: The kayak across Loch Quoich will stick in the wrong part of my memory. I felt out of my comfort zone for the whole crossing. The wind was trying to pull the nose of my kayak round to the left. This was exacerbated by the rear of the boat being relatively fixed in the water by the keel. Rather paradoxically, I found it easier to keep a straight line with the keel up. I tried to keep facing into the wind which seemed to involve paddling almost exclusively with my left arm. My inelegant progress was accompanied by a constant fear of being caught by a gust of wind and tipped into the icy water. It was a big relief to reach the other side, and I was delighted to be left stranded, miles from civilisation, but at least on 'dry' land. Having said that I also felt quite tired. I had exerted myself a lot more than I expected.

Craig: We regrouped on the south bank. The runners ran off and Jamie and I swapped into the sleek, fast sea kayaks and towed our boats back across. 'Tow' is too strong a word really, we steered the play boats as the wind briskly blew them home. In fact, I stopped paddling at one point and my boat blew past upside down, and towed me!

As well as lending us their boats, Kirsty's parents very kindly fed us on our return. My other friend Neil arrived, and the three of us headed to Loch Arkaig to await Paul and Jason.

Jason: After regrouping on the far side, a very relieved Paul and I set off up Sgurr Mor (1003m). The north-west approach was pleasant enough as we were sheltered from the wind until just before the summit, but it was a different story once on the ridge.

We ran along the ridge, over Garbh Chioch Mhor (1013m) and up Sgurr na Ciche (1040m) in storm force winds and horizontal hail. We tried to stick to the more sheltered side of the ridge, but even so Paul discovered a Buff does little to protect your face from being peppered by hail. As we came off Sgurr na Ciche we crossed a raging torrent that would normally be a gently burbling stream. Lower down the rivers were in spate and completely uncrossable. We were thankful to descend into the bog that is Glen Dessarry without such an obstacle, and made our way to the waiting cyclists. We were very relieved to see mountain bikers waiting for us at the house at the top end of the track.

Craig: By the time we arrived at Loch Arkaig the weather had closed in again, and the mountains foiled our attempts at 'tracker watch'. We were a little concerned about having talked our friends into a perilous open water crossing, then deserting them, cold and wet, on the shores of a loch in a storm. We were worried that we might hear about them on the news rather than ever see them again. To ease our collective guilt, after leaving the van by the outflow of Loch Arkaig, we decided to take a car to the end of the road and head up into Glen Dessarry to wait for them there. Neil and Jamie took bikes for the cycle out, but I was on foot. Fortunately, some time later, two cold, wet runners pitched up and by this time they were travelling so slowly that even I could keep up. Jamie and Neil packed Rabbie onto mountain bikes and headed off back to our car park campsite, whilst I packed the runners into a warm car and chauffeured them to the food, drink and mobile accommodation.

Jason: At the head of Loch Arkaig we met up with John who laid out the plan for the coming days, which was get to Glen Feshie by the following night, doing as many Archies as possible en route, then an early start for a big day in the Cairngorms the day after.

Craig: Paul was aghast; Rabbie was going to have to rest for the night again! 'He needs to get to Fersit!' he beseeched. 'There's no one there yet, Paul,' we replied. 'No one expected to be able to cover so much ground today and the fresh legs won't arrive until tomorrow morning.' 'But how will he get there by the morning?' he worried. I agreed to set an alarm and cycle him over in the morning and Paul finally relented and passed out asleep.

Craig, Jamie and Jason by Loch Quioch. Photo: Paul Fettes

DAY 9
7 June 2015
6 ARCHIES

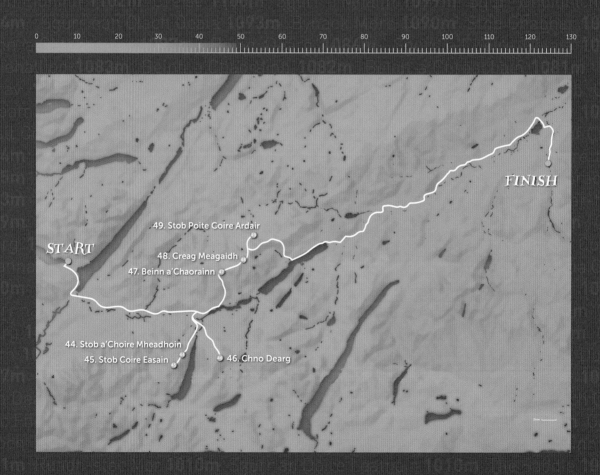

START

FINISH

49. Stob Poite Coire Ardair

48. Creag Meagaidh

47. Beinn a'Chaorainn

44. Stob a'Choire Mheadhoin

45. Stob Coire Easain

46. Chno Dearg

ARKAIG TO FERSIT ROAD CYCLE

Craig Cumming. 29km (560m)

EASAINS

44. Stob a'Choire Mheadhoin (1105m), 45. Stob Coire Easain (1115m): John Irving & Graeme Gatherer. 16km (1200m) 46. Chno Dearg (1046m): Graeme Gatherer & Phil Lacoux. 12km (800m)

ROAD CYCLE

Cycle to Creag Megaidh Tom Fardon. 8km (150m)

CREAG MEAGAIDH TRIO

47. Beinn a'Chaorainn (1052m), 48. Creag Meagaidh (1128m), 49. Stob Poite Coire Ardair (1054m): Tom MacEwan & Alan Carson. 25km (1370m)

ROAD CYCLE

Cycle to Loch Laggan to Glen Feshie: Tom Fardon. 58km (330m)

---

*Distance in kilometres, (and ascent in metres – this is the cumulative ascent of the leg, even if there is a net descent and the finish is lower than the start). In some cases there was a walk (or run) in or out to the start or finish of a leg without carrying the baton.

Arkaig to Fersit cycle link
By Craig Cumming

After a shortcut through the Achnacarry estate, and an enjoyable ride up the bank of the Spean, I passed Rabbie over to Phil Lacoux who was enjoying an early morning cuppa in the car park at Fersit whilst waiting for the rest of the fresh legs to arrive. Shortly after, as I headed back down the road, I was passed by what can be best described as John Irving and two car loads of lurchers who needed to get out and run. That rabbit's going to have a hard day, I thought.

Easains
By Graeme Gatherer – with John Irving

My chance to help guide Rabbie safely over some Archies came at the start of the second week. A rendezvous at Fersit in Glen Spean prompted a quick discussion as to who was doing what, and then we were off... John Irving and I made good progress over Stob a'Choire Mheadhoin and Stob Coire Easain in a stiff breeze with just some light snow in the wind. On our descent we met a group of runners including Jon Ascroft out on a recce for a forthcoming attempt at the Ramsay Round (he went on to smash the record and complete the run for the first time under 17 hours – an incredible solo feat).

Linking the Easains – Graeme Gatherer and John Irving. Photos: Graeme Gatherer

Chno Dearg
By Phil Lacoux and Graeme Gatherer

Phil: The van ceased to keep the wind off me once I clambered out of it after seeing Graeme and John coming down from the Easains. I was surprised that Graeme did not want to pause; a bit worried by a passing comment about this being a training run for a 'Round Mount Blanc' race; embarrassed by early mention of there being no need to dodge the puddles as there will be quite a few; charmed by the careful map checking up and down the route whilst in reality waiting for me; in agreement with his 'just keep moving even if it is not very fast' attitude; and happy to enjoy gentle glissades as part of the descent. Overall I was pleased with my small contribution to a fine venture on a blustery day in a location new to me.

Graeme: On return to the car park a quick partner swap was made and then it was back uphill again to climb Chno Dearg this time with Phil Lacoux. Unfortunately we endured bog most of the way and as temperatures slowly rose we found ourselves in a constant fine misty drizzle. I think Phil was very glad of our swift descent on a big snowfield to outflank the slippery boulder field we had climbed through on the way up. A quick handover to Tom Fardon on the farm track and he duly sped off up the road on his cyclo-cross bike, definitely dressed to impress with his funky sunglasses and full COG Velo* cycle kit. For me it had been a 17-mile day and was rounded off with a team lunch in Dalwhinnie. Not a place you'd expect to find a good bowl of seafood chowder, but it ticked all the boxes at the time! * Carse of Gowrie Cycling Club

Phil Lacoux on Chno Dearg. Photo: Graeme Gatherer

Creag Meagaidh trio

By Tom MacEwan – with Alan Carson

Climbing Munros (ahem, sorry, I mean Archies) while being tracked by GPS is a very disconcerting experience. Wandering around in a whiteout on the summit plateau of Creag Meagaidh I was acutely aware that mission control in Carrbridge would be wondering what on earth we were doing. Alternatively, perhaps they would be oblivious to our travails and tucking into vast quantities of pies to replenish fat and glycogen reserves much depleted by mammoth efforts in the preceding week. The team had set a very high bar, and we knew the clock was ticking. We were supposed to be running over three Archies, and the problem was that we were not absolutely sure that either of the small cairns we had already touched actually constituted this summit. We were also wary of straying too far over the snow dome towards the cornices. Fortunately, closer scrutiny of the map showed that the first cairn was the summit, so we glissaded/stumbled onwards. All of this GPS-tracked confusion in the mist was compounded by the fact that it was the 7th of June, and it was supposed to be summer!

During planning we had volunteered for this particular weekend of Archie's Mountain Challenge, but severe storms had impeded progress and the team were still in Knoydart. However, our call-up came on the Saturday evening – 'Be at Fersit for 08:00 tomorrow!' So it was up at 04:00 to drive from Aberdeen and Edinburgh, respectively, to meet John Irving, Tom Fardon, Phillippe Lacoux and Graeme Gatherer with whom we divided up the day. I liked John's summing up of the planning for an impromptu day involving an awkward bunch of Archies halfway between Knoydart and the Cairngorms as, 'It's a combination of meticulous organisation and ad hoc improvisation.'

We initially spent a pleasant six hours chatting and watching the rain sweep by in sheets while runners ticked off three Archies either side of Loch Treig – the Easains and Chno Dearg – and Tom cycled the stretch from Fersit to our starting point. So, at 14:00 Alan and I set off through the forest on the north side of the A86 at Roughburn. Our first Archie, Beinn a'Chaorainn (1052m) was a wet, boggy ascent with wonderful views (during a brief lull in the dreichness), over the Loch Treig hills, the Grey Corries and the Aonachs. It was amazing to crest the ridge and run up extensive snow fields with massive cornices to our right. The summit came quite easily and we, to paraphrase Wainwright, 'paused awhile to take selfies with a rabbit.'

Alan Carson on Beinn a'Chaorainn with Loch Treig, the Eassains and the Grey Corries in the background. Photo: Tom MacEwan

The descent to the bealach west of Creag Meagaidh was pretty uneventful and, as we climbed and the mists closed in, the rusting fence posts of an old boundary were a welcome sight, at least to those of us from the FTF (Follow the Fence) school of navigation as this boundary was marked on the map. Unfortunately, the higher fence posts have disintegrated, which partly explains our brief disorientation on the plateau. Once we had established, after five minutes of faffing, that we had conquered our second Archie, the mighty Creag Meagaidh (1130m), the descent to the Window involved a bit of doglegged navigation. This was followed by a quick burst up to our third summit, Stob Poite Coire Ardair (1053m). After a few more photos of Rabbie and some revoltingly snottery selfies we retraced our steps to the Window, in the hope of an easy descent. (We could have continued along the ridge to bag the final Munro of the group, but hey; Munros are so 'last Millennium'.)

Unfortunately, our 'easy descent' hopes were quickly dashed, as the east face of the Window was almost completely choked with a bank of quite hard-packed snow which was much too steep to descend without ice axes. We picked our way down the side of the snowfield on broken scree and loose turf, then followed the glen to the Nature Reserve car park, passing snow bridges over the burn and then through a young woodland of rowan and birches. As the sun eventually came out for the evening we were joined by John and Tom, the latter possibly anxious to complete his cycle to Glen Feshie, and we finished by about 19:00.

It was a fantastic privilege to have taken part in the Challenge, and following the tracker in the week before and after our stage was enthralling. I was relieved to see that there is only a slight kink in our tracked passage across the summit plateau of Creag Meagaidh.

DAY 10
8 June 2015
16 ARCHIES

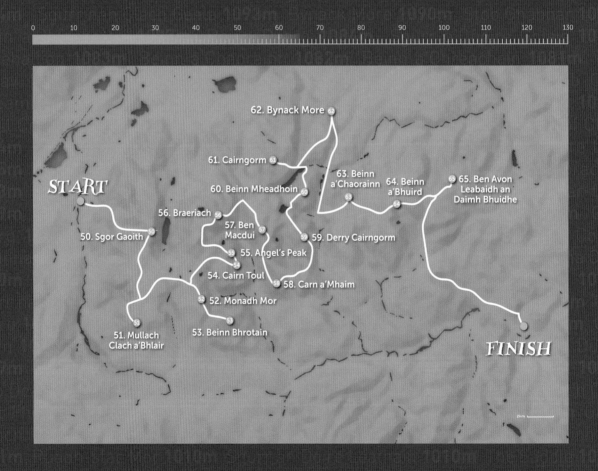

62. Bynack More

61. Cairngorm

63. Beinn a'Chaorainn

64. Beinn a'Bhuird

65. Ben Avon Leabaidh an Daimh Bhuidhe

60. Beinn Mheadhoin

START

56. Braeriach

57. Ben Macdui

50. Sgor Gaoith

59. Derry Cairngorm

55. Angel's Peak

54. Cairn Toul

58. Carn a'Mhaim

52. Monadh Mor

51. Mullach Clach a'Bhlair

53. Beinn Bhrotain

FINISH

2km

GLEN FESHIE TO LAIRIG GHRU

50. Sgor Gaoith (1118m), 51. Mullach Clach a'Bhlair (1019m), 52. Monadh Mor (1113m), 53. Beinn Bhrotain (1157m), 54. Cairn Toul (1291m), 55. Angel's Peak (1258m), 56. Braeriach (1296m): Russell Duncan & Jason Hardy. 47km (1720m), walk out 9km

LAIRIG GHRU TO CAIRNGORM

57. Ben Macdui (1309m), 58. Carn a'Mhaim (1037m), 59. Derry Cairngorm (1155m), 60. Beinn Mheadhoin (1182m): John Irving & Tom Fardon. 27km (1890m) after 9km walk in

SUMMIT HANDOVER

61. Cairngorm (1245m): John Irving, Tom Fardon, Steve Manning, Paul Fettes, Amy Manning & Pepper the dog

CAIRNGORM TO DEESIDE

62. Bynack More (1090m), 63. Beinn a'Chaorainn (1083m), 64. Beinn a'Bhuird (1197m), 65. Ben Avon – Leabaidh an Daimh Bhuidhe (1171m): Steve Manning & Paul Fettes. 31km (1460m). 4km walk in, 3km walk out.

MOUNTAIN BIKE

Down to Deeside road: Amy Manning, Jamie Smith & Craig Cumming. 5km.

*Distance in kilometres, (and ascent in metres – this is the cumulative ascent of the leg, even if there is a net descent and the finish is lower than the start). In some cases there was a walk (or run) in or out to the start or finish of a leg without carrying the baton.

Western Cairngorms: Glen Feshie to Lairig Ghru
By Russell Duncan – with Jason Hardy

Conditions were finally improving. The spectre of three big legs in the Cairngorms loomed and we hoped to cross the entire range in 24 hours.

Glen Feshie, 4am. Two of us started the AMC Cairngorm assault. It was a lovely run up to Sgor Gaoith and as we neared the summit the terrain remained good; so did our legs, but the overhead was not great with cloud sitting at about 900m. That was less than ideal when trying to find the tops of seven mountains over 1000m, but hey, it wasn't snowing – yet. We had done a good recce of the route beforehand and were rewarded for this as we hoovered up the ground between Sgor Gaoith, Carn Ban Mor and Mullach Clach a'Bhlair. Jay kept us right whenever I tried to take a path. 'Paul wouldn't like this if he's watching the tracker, let's just go straight across the bog,' he said.

Mullach Clach a'Bhlair to Monadh Mor and our legs still felt good. 'This is going to be just fine,' we thought to ourselves as we high-fived our way across the top of our first three Archies of the day. Onto Beinn Bhrotain, which is where we started to feel the effects of the first 25km. The rocky ascent is steep out of the narrow bealach from Monadh Mor and we slogged it up there, but were still sprightly enough to enjoy some photographic antics at the summit cairn. The view south was tremendous and we saw where hoped to be in 24 hours. We also saw our first glimpses of Cairn Toul, The Angel's Peak and Braeriach. 'Nae bather,' we said, but the previous 30km had taken their toll. We kept going but the terrain was getting tough, with large boulders and minimal beaten track. The weather also deteriorated, and we were treated to the view of a wintry looking storm approaching from the west. We opted to ascend the shoulder that goes up Angel's Peak before contouring south to Cairn Toul and climbed this fourth highest Archie in a blizzard. That seemed fitting given the prevailing conditions recently, but we and the AMC wider team were ready for a change and it was on the way.

Paul 10:16am by text:

> you are doing really well but going up Angels peak rather than Cairn Toul...

Our mild mannered response:

> Calm your pants. It's horrible up here.

Cairn Toul and Angel's Peak from Braeriach. Photo: Jason Hardy

We tracked back to The Angel's Peak then pressed on to Braeriach (which was farther than it needed to be or we wanted it to be) but the weather was changing. Cold, thick cloud gave way to lovely sunshine and a blue sky. We rejoiced and gorged ourselves on photos of us standing on snow with the blue sky above us, before taking a snifter of Eden gin and hot footing it down the snowfield in one of Braeriach's eastern corries. 'You were moving so fast it looked like you were on skis,' Tom told us afterwards, and we shook his hand gratefully as we handed over Rabbie several times for the benefit of *the Adventure Show* cameraman who was waiting with Tom and John Irving at the Pools of Dee. 'Only a 12km walk out to the car, lads.' We had already done 40+km but knew that we still had a wee job to do to get our burger and chips. Still, rather that than bash on up Ben Macdui!

Russell ordering beers from near the summit of Braeriach. Photo: Jason Hardy

Jay and I are long past worrying about seeing each other battered and bruised, which is just as well because as we neared the end of our epic day in the Cairngorms we were pretty spent. 'That was good though Jay, wasn't it?' I mused as we approached the Sugarbowl car park. 'Yeah mate, that was pretty good. Shall we go and pick up your car from Glen Feshie now?' 'Suppose we ought to!' Beer was in the post, but it would have to wait another hour...

Central Cairngorms: Ben Macdui to Cairgorm
By Tom Fardon and John Irving

John: Things could be worse. Luxury accommodation had been provided in the Duncan-Hardy holiday mansion in Carrbridge. Tom and I awoke at a civilised hour, and logged on to the tracker. The lads had crossed the Moine Mhor to Ben Bhrotain at great speed. Would there be time for the full breakfast? It might be tight getting to the Pools of Dee at the top of the Lairig Ghru, but they couldn't fail to cross our path on their way down. We went for it; slow release of pork fat from a stuffed stomach is underrated these days as a fuelling strategy for endurance exercise, but I find it reliable. We talked through the plan, sipping a second cappuccino. 20 miles and 6000 feet would take us round five Archies in a big loop of the Cairngorms. Weather was clear and sometimes sunny, but not hot. It was going to be a good day, contemplated without apprehension.

Tom: Our day in the limelight. John and I drove to the Sugarbowl car park, just below the Cairngorm ski centre, and met our companion for the first part of the day — Dominic, the cameraman for *The Adventure Show*. The rendezvous point was the Pools of Dee, at the crest of the Lairig Ghru. As we had a few hours to get there, Dominic was very keen to get some 'action footage' of us running up the mountains — this meant running the same stretch repeatedly so Dominic could get wide angle shots, close ups, and those 'from low down on the floor' shots that *The Adventure Show* always seems so keen on.

John: We settled into trotting along the path to the Chalamain Gap, and stopping for filming from different angles. Tom and I had not been out together on the hill before. I knew him as well as one can from chats at Parkrun, and adjacent clinics in Arbroath Infirmary. His athletic credentials were well established as a doyen of Monifeith Triathlon Club, and Parkrun director. He was dressed for racing with full body Lycra, wrap around shades, and logo encrusted baseball cap. I shuffled alongside in shorts and fleece. I had a good few miles in my legs, having survived gale force rain and snow on the Highlander Mountain Marathon and the Islands Peaks Race a few weeks earlier. It was a surprise when Tom told me that every feature of my gait was the precise opposite of everything he trained people to do in triathlons. While I was unsure about how relevant this observation would be I reflected that it was good to establish such clear communication and teamwork so early in the day.

Tom: At the top of the Chalamain Gap was another camera man, there to carry out interviews. I think they were probably after some short, sharp soundbites, but instead they got two doctors rambling on about the beauty of the Cairgorms and the ludicrous nature of the Scottish summer, just as it started to snow.

John: I burbled away happily, Tom kept his shades on. On again into the Lairig Ghru and no sign of Russell / Jason. Conditions were perfect for running, and the pace was gentle. We walked up the steep and broken ground and trotted along the smoother stretches of path. We were into the boulder field in no time, and picked out separate ways to the lochans. Tibetan prayer flags fluttered in hippy transgression of littering laws. The wind ruffled the dark surfaces, and we hunkered down behind some boulders in a patch of sun. Conversation slowed. Out of sight on the Braeriach plateau, the tracker was pinging out a satellite signal to the watching world on office monitors, but not to us. We had nothing to do but wait. Loitering in the hills for an unknown interval is a privilege that is hard to obtain; we enjoyed every moment. Then Russell and Jason crested the skyline and interrupted the daydreams.

Tom: We met Russell and Jay at the Pools of Dee. They ran over to us, then they ran back to do it again once Dominic had the cameras rolling. Twenty minutes of wide angles, close ups, and 'running past the camera' shots, and we were off, with Rabbie in our backpack and five Archies to climb before bedtime. John's idea of 'cracking on' was to run up Ben Macdui from the south-west, up the steepest approach. A baptism of fire for someone who's never climbed a Munro before; with the camera filming us, we started to climb. 'Shouldn't we head for the path?' I suggested. 'The beaten path is for beaten men,' he replied.

John: The rising traverse from the Lairig Ghru is not well travelled; there was no hint of a path, but it is a superb route. Steep enough to be interesting, and the views change rapidly, opening out massively to the Devil's Point and beyond. Dominic had been uncertain about following us up to Ben Macdui with Health and Safety Rules discouraging solo high mountain travel when working. He was delighted with the pictures, running strongly on ahead, filming us from both sides and capturing the Cairngorms as the opposite of rounded bouldery puddings. With all the distractions,

Tom Fardon crossing the Loch Avon outflow. Photo: John Irving

time flew and the summit of Ben Macdui arrived. Filming finished with us heading over the horizon to Carn a'Mhaim.

Tom: After the first pitch we were able to pick up the pace a bit, and run up to the summit. Then we went back so Dominic could get the reverse angle. And again from behind. The same off the top. He left us to it at that point, and ran back to his car. I hope he had the lens cap off.

John: Long days often feel easy for the first half, and then don't feel easy again. The descent to the col is 1700 feet of rocky scree and short diversions onto snow lying over the Allt Clach nan Taillear. This flowed more smoothly than we did. The ridge to Carn a'Mhaim is a grand highway, and more snow runnels took us down steeply to below Derry Cairngorm. This is when the effort started. Two thousand feet of ascent of windless, midgey, deep heather was the psychological crux of the day. Fatigue held us back, chat a required distraction. Bad holiday jobs were recalled and revelled in, and we ground back up to the summits.

Tom: The rest of the day is a blur. Carn a'Mhaim gave us an amazing view of where we'd been, and what we were about to do. When John suggested we run down the snow bank to cut across to Derry Cairngorm, I thought he was joking – apparently not. We'd watched Russell and Jay do a similar trick off the top of Braeriach, and it proved to be a genius idea – descending, or falling, with style. We were then given the 'option' of climbing Beinn Mheadhoin – which meant, of course, that we would do it, to save those who came after us (Steve and Paul) from having to do it.

John: Duke of Edinburgh groups were camped at Loch Etchachan, still too full of energy to sit in quiet contemplation. We trotted past and onto the steep shoulder of Beinn Mheadhoin. The pace steadied and rolled onto the flatter ridge. The northerly wind chilled more deeply in the brief showers, summit rewards were required a mile early as the waterproofs went on.

Tom: Just before the summit, John pulled out a bag of Peanut M&Ms. I hugged him.

The descent from Beinn Mheadhoin to the outflow of Loch Avon was tough on my knees, but the scenery got better and better. John had mentioned the possibility of 'crossing a river at some point'. I hadn't realised that this meant wading across the waist-deep, ice-cold outflow of a mountain loch. But we kept Rabbie's feet dry, and pushed on towards Cairngorm.

John: Snow and rainbows led down to the Loch Avon outflow and the base of the final climb. Seracs perched on the slabs and we crept underneath. Tom was delighted with the altimeter setting on his Garmin and called out the passing of every 50m.

Tom: As we approached the summit of Cairngorm, we broke into a canter, just in time to see Paul and Steve waiting at the summit, with Amy and Pepper the dog. I have rarely been so happy to see the finish line of an event.

John: Suddenly we were on top, with Paul and Steve and Amy grinning in the early evening light, their timing spot on. Rays of sunbeams picked out Aviemore. We had put in a good shift.

Tom: I've done a fair bit of running, off road and on trails, half marathons at a decent lick, but I've never done anything as tough as climbing those five Archies. The walk down to the ski centre was painful – iliotibial bands like banjo strings. But the elation of knowing I'd taken Rabbie over a big chunk of the Cairngorms in the previous 10 hours made it all worthwhile. As did the promise of a curry back in Carrbridge.

Tom Fardon on Beinn Mheadhoin; Cairngorm Rabbie. Photos: John Irving

From Cairngorm to Deeside
and from Formality to Friendship

By Paul Fettes with Steve Manning

(with contributions from Amy Manning and Craig Cumming)

Paul: Standing on the top of Cairngorm, Scotland's sixth highest mountain, I felt refreshed and ready for the long run ahead. Most of the previous 24 hours had passed in a very pleasant blur of inactivity. I had enjoyed some 'down time' in Russell's Carrbridge house, eating, drinking, sleeping and partaking in relaxed conversation with the rest of the team. Wi-Fi and a landline had finally enabled me to check the flurry of emails, texts and Facebook entries related to the Challenge, but I was also able to step outside the Archie bubble and catch up with my wife Heidi, and with news headlines in a world from which I had been isolated for a week, although in some ways it seemed more like a lifetime. I had also been able to enjoy a full cooked breakfast in The Carrbridge Kitchen, the thought of which had kept a bedraggled me going at the end of my run with Jason through Glen Dessarry and out of Knoydart.

Handover on the summit of Cairngorm, with Amy, Tom, Steve and John. Photo: Paul Fettes

Steve and a pregnant Amy Manning appeared in their camper van around lunchtime. At the time, Steve was an anaesthetic registrar in the same department as me, and every time he had worked with me, he had called me 'Doctor Fettes', to which I would reply 'Just call me Paul'. He had obviously discussed this with Amy because when he arrived he said 'Hello Doctor Fettes... Oh no! That's a pound to ARCHIE already!' Instead of a 'Swear Box' they had decided that he should have an 'Unnecessarily Formal Title for Your Running Partner' box instead, which at this rate could cost him a lot of money!

Amy: My husband, Steve, had told me about the Challenge which some of his colleagues were organising. Anaesthetists have a certain reputation and this certainly fitted with it. The challenge interested me as I had been involved in a similar journey as a child. My Dad, Hugh Symonds, had completed all the Munros in one continuous journey back in 1990. As a young girl I followed him with rest of my family in the back of a camper van. I was excited to be able to take part in another journey which I would remember this time! So, we booked a week's holiday and made ourselves available. We had a yellow VW camper van so could be available anywhere, anytime, which was lucky as the Challenge was fairly fluid. A portable bed would be very handy.

The only complicating factor was that I was due to be around 20 weeks pregnant when the Challenge started. My aim was to remain pretty active during pregnancy but I wasn't sure that running in the hills would be possible or wise. But cycling wasn't a problem, so I offered my services for carrying Rabbie, the baton, between the mountains.

Jason Hardy
June 7, 2015

Now that is what kept me going yesterday. Full Scottish breakfast at the Carrbridge Kitchen. They now do burgers at lunch time. That's you and me tomorrow Russell Duncan

👍 7

👍 Like   ↗ Share

Paul: With the luxury of being able to watch Rabbie's progress through the Cairngorms on the tracker, we set off at an appropriate time to meet Tom and John. As Amy drove us up to the Cairngorm ski car park in the Manning-mobile, Steve asked to see the route. I pulled the map out of my sack to show him, only to discover that I had the wrong map! I had assumed that our route would be on my double sided Cairngorm Explorer Map, but as far as that was concerned we would be running off the edge, and into uncharted territory! I am rather embarrassed to say that to rectify this problem we had to stop in Aviemore and buy a new map. The Carrbridge respite had clearly made me 'take my eye off the ball'.

From the ski car park Steve and I, accompanied by Amy and Pepper the dog, made our way up the hill on a track beside the funicular railway. When we reached the top station, we stopped in the shelter of the Ptarmigan Restaurant. It was now early evening and the building was closed, but the walls emanated a Wi-Fi signal as well as giving shelter. We could check Tom and John's progress by following the tracker, and this allowed us to engineer perfect timing for the only summit handover of the

Challenge, on Cairngorm. After 'the obligatory summit selfie' we said goodbye to Amy and a tired but happy pair of runners, and headed off into the... well, thankfully, the sun wasn't setting quite yet, but we knew it would before we got to Deeside. It was cool and grey, but the cloud was high and visibility was excellent as we floated over arctic tundra and skimmed down enormous snowfields to The Saddle which overlooks Loch Avon at the top of Strath Nethy. From there we followed a good path up a gentle ridge to A'Choinneach and enjoyed amazing views to the north as we ran over an easy plateau to Bynack More (1090m). We made a rather undignified descent through deep heather on the steep east side of the mountain before joining a good track which led past the Refuge at the Fords of Avon. I think we rather startled a couple who were making their evening meal there as we trotted past, hardly slowing as we skipped over the stepping stones that led over the icy waters of the River Avon.

From there we followed the path due south before leaving it to contour round the southern slopes of Beinn a'Chaorainn, with the intention of avoiding the top and going eastwards towards Beinn a'Bhuird. For some reason I had forgotten that Beinn a'Chaorrainn (1083m) was one of our allotted Archie summits, and it was fortunate that Steve questioned me about this at the time that he did. A very short detour later, we were at the top of our third Archie of the day. That was twice now that Steve had questioned me at a vital moment, and saved us a lot of time and embarrassment. Concentrate, Paul! I realised that I had failed to plan properly for this route, and I was thankful that Steve had the sense to question my judgement.

Steve is a great guy and it was good to spend some time with him outside work. Originally from Whitley Bay, Steve is an exceptionally talented sportsman. He has played professional rugby for Wasps, and has competed in triathlons at international level. His wife Amy is also an amazing athlete and would have taken a fuller part in the Challenge if she were not pregnant. Sister of Joe, she is a member of the Symonds family, who are legendary in fell-running circles (more on that later) and I found it ironic that husband Steve is regarded as the 'fat boy' of the Symonds family!

Our trek from Beinn a'Chaorrainn to Beinn a'Bhuird in the fading light was slower. We had to pick our way over boulders, through patches of thick heather and across the rather mountainous peat bog of Moine Bhealaidh. The top of Beinn a'Bhuird (1197m) was shrouded in mist and as we approached the summit plateau it became completely dark.

'Table hill' is aptly named because it is pancake flat at the top. In poor torch-lit visibility, we followed my compass bearing through the murk. I was confident we were very close to the top, but we could not find it. I was grateful to have a GPS mapping app on my phone, without which I think we might have circled for a while. I had precious little battery power left, so after finding the summit I turned the phone back off, and relied on traditional methods of route finding to find our way towards Ben Avon. We followed a compass bearing heading roughly due east. We knew that if we headed too far to the left (north) we would hit a cliff edge, dropping into Garbh Choire. There was practically no wind and even in the dark we could sense the wind from the corrie, and this helped us navigate uneventfully down to the col.

Steve Manning with Loch Avon in the background. Photo: Paul Fettes

As we descended we came out of the cloud, and were rewarded with moonlight as we made our way up easy ground to the granite tors on the summit of Ben Avon, Leabaidh an Daimh Bhuidhe (1171m). Climbing over these giant moonlit rock structures was a precarious but strangely gratifying experience. We could see lights of Deeside villages twinkling in the distance. All we had to do now was find our way down. For some reason we were feeling a little weary by this point, and the way out was a real struggle. We headed south-west off the top of Ben Avon, down an achingly steep slope on tired legs to Glas Allt Mor. Once we reached the stream we made our painful way south on a good path. Our destination in the grounds of Invercauld House by the River Dee still seemed a long way away. Thankfully as we approached a ruin about halfway down, we were met by the very welcome sight of my friend and colleague, Craig Cumming.

Craig: We had a plan to make life easier for Paul and Steve. Jamie Smith and I were to meet them as they descended the Grampians, at a ruin on the path north of Braemar, and cycle Rabbie out. Amy Manning arrived in her camper van and met us at the car park before we headed up the hill. Being pregnant, Amy was concerned that she'd hold us up, but as she'd chosen a cyclo-cross bike, was wearing what looked suspiciously like British team kit, and was married to Steve, we were more worried that it would be the other way around.

We set off with bikes and good lights into the dark and were soon at the ruin, which was a little beyond the point where the track was easily navigable by bike and a little before the point where the landscape opens up again and you can see up the mountain. Mobile reception had let us down again, so Jamie waited with Amy while I walked a short way up the path, turned off my light and waited to look for lights and listen for voices in the darkness.

A good while later a patch of 'not quite so dark' appeared on the mountainside and this eventually resolved itself into a patch of light followed by a rather weary Paul and Steve. We exchanged greetings, and a damp rabbit was carried down the hill by the fresh members of the team, leaving the tired ones to walk out. Once back at the car park we drove a vehicle back up the road (fortunately there were no locked gates that night on the estate roads) to recover the weary travellers.

Steve Manning on top of Bynack More. Photo: Paul Fettes

Paul: In less than 24 hours, over three legs we had traversed the Cairngorms from Glen Feshie to Deeside via 16 Archies. Steve and I had covered 40km with 2000m ascent in about six hours. I think it was about 3am by the time we got to bed, and I slept like a baby. The following day, Heidi very kindly drove up to collect me and take me back to Dundee for my only day away from the Challenge. As I left, Steve gave me a big hug. I had enjoyed spending time with Steve. It is impossible to go through an experience like our run without forming some sort of lasting bond, and I would like to think that we will remain on first name terms from now on. From formality to friendship felt like real progress!

DAY 11
9 June 2015
10 ARCHIES

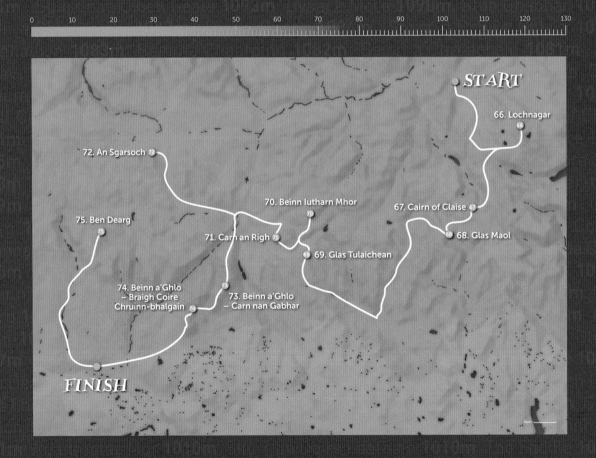

0   10   20   30   40   50   60   70   80   90   100   110   120   130

START

66. Lochnagar

72. An Sgarsoch

70. Beinn Iutharn Mhor

67. Cairn of Claise

75. Ben Dearg

71. Carn an Righ

68. Glas Maol

69. Glas Tulaichean

74. Beinn a'Ghlo
– Braigh Coire
Chruinn-bhalgain

73. Beinn a'Ghlo
– Carn nan Gabhar

FINISH

DEESIDE TO GLENSHEE

66. Lochnagar (1155m), 67. Cairn of Claise (1064m), 68. Glas Maol (1068m): Tom Fardon & John Irving. 31km (1460m), 3km walk out

CYCLE

Cycle down to Spittal of Glenshee: Craig Cumming & Jamie Smith 11km (50m)

SPITTAL OF GLENSHEE TO FALLS OF TARF

69. Glas Tulaichean (1051m), 70. Beinn Iutharn Mhor (1045m), 71. Carn an Righ (1029m): Matthew McCullagh & Russell Duncan. 3km cycle (60m), 23km run (1420m). 19km cycle out (370m).

FALLS OF TARF TO BLAIR ATHOLL

72. An Sgarsoch (1006m), 73. Beinn a'Ghlo – Carn nan Gabhar (1121m), 74. Beinn a'Ghlo – Braigh Coire Chruinn-bhalgain (1070m): Calum Grant & Steve Manning. 35km (1950m), after 19km cycle in (620m)

BEN DEARG

75. Ben Dearg (1008m): David Henderson & Mike Donald. 30km (1064m).

*Distance in kilometres, (and ascent in metres – this is the cumulative ascent of the leg, even if there is a net descent and the finish is lower than the start). In some cases there was a walk (or run) in or out to the start or finish of a leg without carrying the baton.

Cairngorm Zombies: Lochnagar to Glenshee

By John Irving and Tom Fardon

"I have no spur to prick the sides of my intent but only vaulting ambition that o'erleaps itself and falls on the other"– Macbeth, in *Macbeth* by William Shakespeare

John: It was 05:30 on the White Mounth, four kilometres west of the summit of Lochnagar, and a beautiful summer morning was slowly getting started. Golden early morning light glowed, birdsong chattered like the shimmer of strings presaging a key moment in a film. The path from the Ballochbuie Forest eased onto the plateau and I turned to Tom Fardon and nodded – it was time to run. Twenty seconds later we stopped. His straight-legged stumble dictated by 'iliotibial bands like banjo strings'; my eccentric, penguin waddle was no faster than walking pace. Two minutes later we tried again with the same result. Sublimity crashed into reality. We were due at Glas Maol, 12 miles west, at 08:00 to hand over the rabbit and we were moving at two miles per hour. The relay chain of colleagues, friends and partial acquaintances stretched virtually into the future, looking at their watches and tutting. How had we gotten ourselves in this mess?

It was my idea to volunteer for the Lochnagar to Glas Maol leg. I knew the ground well and relished the idea of a dawn-lit lope over the undulating plateau to Glen Shee. Russell Duncan had phoned me the previous Thursday morning. I was in tidy-up mode at work after an emergency case in the small hours, caffeinated into activity. We sat in the ironically named 'fresh air' garden of Ninewells Hospital among the cigarette butts and the trees. He had the news from the west. The team was stretched thin, and unsure of timings with rising river levels in Knoydart. The plan was to fix the long and committing Cairngorm legs for fresh runners, giving enough time to make slow progress in the west. We could fill up spare time bagging the peaks around Creag Meagaidh. It all made practical sense, and I agreed. He offered accommodation in Carrbridge and I accepted. He suggested that he would quite like to do the Glen Feshie to Braeriach leg, following the next day by Glas Tulaichean. Such reasonable requests could not be denied. I was keen for the central Cairngorms and for Lochnagar. That left a short recovery time in between. Nevermind. It'll be fine.

Tom Fardon
June 9, 2015

The view from Lochnagar this morning. Stunning way to spend a few hours on a Tuesday.

Sorry we took so long - someone got the estimate 'a bit' off (John Irving...)

👍 6

👍 Like   ↪ Share

Back at Carrbridge after our Cairngorm exploits, curry and beers had partially restored the inner men. Tom needed to download the day onto Strava to prove it had happened. I needed to get to bed. Two hours' sleep and it would be time for day two.

Tom: The alarm went off at 02:30. By 03:00 we were back on the road, heading for Invercauld Bridge, to collect Rabbie from the MTB riders who had ferried him from the foot of Ben Avon.

John: The drive round past Tomintoul was steady, we picked a cuddly rabbit off a camper van step as planned and headed into the hills.

Tom: By 04:30 we were back 'running', through the forest, and up to start the climb to Lochnagar. The previous night we had made a number of guesstimates as to how long it would take us to get round Lochnagar, Cairn of Claise and Glas Maol – anything from 2½ hours to 4½ hours. John told me to think of it as 'just an undulating half marathon'. We hit the top of Lochnagar at 2 hours 28. It was going to be a longer day on the hill than we thought. But what a way to spend a Tuesday morning. We were at the summit at 07:00. We had not seen anyone else on the mountain, it felt as though we were the only people in the Highlands, and the view from the top was magical.

John Irving enjoying the view from the top of Lochnagar. Photo: Tom Fardon

John: I had described the day as an undulating half marathon, conveniently ignoring the five-mile trek to get to the first summit, and the fact that we might be a little tired when we started. Lochnagar (1155m) was bright and smiling. From there we undulated over the short grass, moss and thin soil as it stopped being early morning. Attempts at running became less frequent and then ceased. The hardest struggle was contouring past the barely protruding pimple of Tolmount – we had to deploy mutual tales of incredibly clever diagnoses made on limited information to keep morale out of the ditch.

Tom: A lesson in 'contouring' got us to Cairn of Claise (1064m), giving us a view of the last climb, Glas Maol (1068m). On the shoulder of Glas Maol, just as 12 hours previously when I was hitting rock bottom, John reached into that Tardis-like rucksack of his and pulled out another packet of Peanut M&Ms. Don't set off up a mountain without a bag of M&Ms.

John: Cairn of Claise marked the watershed, and Glas Maol followed. Thankfully Jamie and Craig had mountain-biked to the top of the tows on Meall Odhar, and we captured a group selfie in sepia. As they sped off down to Glenshee with Rabbie safely ensconced in a pack, our job was done.

A Grand Day Oot: Glenshee to the Falls of Tarf

By Matthew McCullagh – with Russell Duncan

I set off from Perth at about 7am, having agreed to meet Russell at the Spittal of Glenshee at 8am. I knew Russell from a previous run in the Lomond Hills several years ago, and knew he was going to be a great running partner. Like so many of the other ARCHIE athletes I met, he is such a positive guy with a beaming smile and a love of the hills that it's easy to feed off his 'keep on keeping on' attitude – just what I needed having shared a particularly tough run with Barry Maguire exactly seven days earlier. Luckily, the weather was set to be warm and sunny with very little wind – it really is amazing how different the conditions were compared to just a week earlier.

We had a bit of time to catch up with each other and chat through our leg before eventually started our shift at about midday, taking Rabbie from Craig and Jamie who had cycled him down to the Spittal from Glenshee ski centre. Being generous souls, Craig and Jamie had agreed to lend Russell and me their bikes to ride up the track as far as Glenlochsie Lodge. I say generous, because this meant them walking along the same track to retrieve their bikes from the where we had 'dumped' them by the lodge. During our brief ride, there was a quirky moment when we crossed a small ford at Glenlochsie Farm. I was leading and didn't want to look like a Jessie by getting off and pushing through the ford, so sped up intending to swoosh through it without a second thought. Unfortunately, I hit a big lump of stone almost as soon as I rode into the water, and ended up sitting in the burn next to my bike (sorry Craig/Jamie!) looking at Russell who was wearing his most patient and 'don't worry – it could happen to anyone' face.

Anyway, we summitted Glas Tulaichean (1051m) without any further trouble. I have to admit a real sense of relief and joy at bagging my first Archie. Whilst at the summit we met a group of hill walkers from Blairgowrie who had been following the challenge in *The Courier*. One of them even had Graeme Gatherer as his GP!

Then on to Beinn Iutharn Mhor (1045m), passing and chatting to a couple of Duke of Edinburgh groups from Edinburgh. Russell was running incredibly well considering he had already put in a really impressive shift the previous day, running seven Archies in the Cairngorms with Jay. At the top of our second Archie, Rabbie did a short Highland dance atop the cairn which we managed to catch on film and post on Facebook later.

Lost again? Jason on the wrong page - checking the map in the western Cairngorms. Photo: Russell Duncan

We retraced our steps off Beinn Iutharn Mhor before swinging west to climb Carn an Righ (1029m). Halfway up the ascent we began to feel the heat and realised that we needed to take on more water than we were averaging to this point if we were to keep sufficiently hydrated, so once we summitted our third and final Archie we headed for a stream source a few hundred metres down, only to find it completely dry. Again, I have to stress the incredible shift in conditions in the seven days since my run with Barry, where we were bog trotting for most of the day and wading through deep snow for the rest. Bonkers!

We eventually found water at Allt a'Ghlinne Bhig on the way to Fealar Lodge, so stopped for a good drink and a look at the map. Then it was a hard slog to our rendezvous with Calum and Steve at the Falls of Tarf. We were both feeling pretty wabbit by this point, so took it in turns to lead and encouraged each other through the last couple of kilometres. Earlier, Russell had used the phrase 'keep on keeping on' which had reminded me of a song of the same name by a band from the '80s called the Redskins. It's a bit of a left-wing rant against Maggie T, but well worth a listen if you get the chance.

We reached Falls of Tarf about 4½ hours after starting off, and met Calum, Steve and the pocket dynamo that is Amy. They had ridden up Glen Tilt from Blair Atholl, so we jumped on their bikes and rode back in the opposite direction. It was a bit of a bumpy ride on tired legs but way better than having to run all the way back.

My one enduring memory of the Challenge was meeting and interacting with so many positive and capable people. I cannot express how humbling it was to watch (on the tracker) team after team putting in such Herculean efforts again and again. Thank you to Paul and everyone else for the opportunity to join one of the most special events I think I have ever taken part in – never has the phrase 'standing on the shoulders of giants' seemed so apt.

Not your usual working day:
Falls of Tarf to Blair Atholl the indirect way,
By Calum Grant – with Steve Manning

It was late afternoon by the time Steve and I met Russell and Matthew by a waterfall, well up in a remote glen somewhere in the Perthshire highlands, and I found it hard to believe that this should have been a normal day at work. Things started to deviate from the norm 24 hours earlier when I received a call at work from my colleague and fellow anaesthetist, Jason Hardy. Although he was technically on holiday, he begged me to take his place in his next leg of the Challenge the following day. In order to free me up, he proposed to come to the hospital and take my place at work. The reason for this proposal was that he was totally wrecked from his big effort in the Cairngorms and considered work the easier and more desirable option! As I guess was the case for many people throughout the event, much of the next 24 hours was spent packing, and trying to confirm arrangements for the stage. I was told to take running kit and a mountain bike, initially to Glenshee then later to Blair Atholl. So after a morning at work, Jason swapped in and I left for the hills. Jason must have been pretty far gone because as I left the hospital car park at around 1pm I couldn't believe my luck – conditions were bluebird-clear, warm, sunny – the kind of day you live for in Scotland.

I had a rough idea what was going on as the tracker map was live on the big screen in the seminar room of our department – and there was plenty of discussion and 'oohs' and 'aahs' at the incredible progress that was being made now that the weather had turned in our favour. I was mightily impressed that overnight the baton had come all the way from the Cairngorms, and over Lochnagar and Glas Maol. I envied the runners coming over those hills. They must have enjoyed a spectacular sunrise – what a buzz! I wanted my fix of the action too – and I certainly wasn't disappointed.

I met Steve and Amy Manning in Blair Atholl. They had both been involved in the monster effort over the Cairngorms, and I was amazed that Steve was so up for our leg – especially when I heard what was involved. The updated plan was that all three of us were going to cycle 20K up Glen Tilt to the Falls of Tarf where we would intercept Russell Duncan and Matthew McCullagh, who were coming over from Glenshee.

They would then cycle out on our bikes to Blair Atholl, leaving Steve and me to run out to An Sgarsoch (which is in the back end of beyond, and in the middle of nowhere), and back over Beinn a'Ghlo to Blair Atholl. Jeepers, I thought, that's a huge run and not only that, we weren't going to get the handover now until after 5pm. It's fair to say I was feeling a bit nervous. It was a big leg, but I also knew that I had to get home to be in some kind of shape to work the following morning. Steve, although a bit fatigued, was relaxed and seemed well up for it. Mentally I decided I would need to embrace the challenge ahead, relax, take it in and just suck it up.

The world is a big place and you get a sense of this when you realise how much of your own small country you've never seen. I had never set eyes or foot (or wheel) on any of this terrain. I can tell you Beinn a'Ghlo is a mighty hill and if you haven't climbed it then, at some point, you must. It's a hill that is remarkably well hidden behind Blair Atholl, especially when you consider its size, and even cycling up Glen Tilt it's not until you get up to the head of the glen and look back to the south that you can see the summit. In fact I think the only place you can really appreciate this hill is from the top. As we cycled up the glen we met several groups of walkers coming out, having enjoyed their day in the hills and the sunshine – yet we were just getting started. I really appreciate that sense of adventure – going against the grain, of doing the improbable, and when others are retreating for home, you're heading into the fray.

With perfect timing we met Russell and Matthew just after they'd arrived at the Falls of Tarf, and I think it's fair to say they were buzzing. They had had a big day with incredible weather, and now they had a relatively leisurely downhill mountain bike back to base to look forward to. I was certainly in a different, more restless, frame of mind. A quick handover and we were off on our way toward An Sgarsoch (1006m), the lonely mountain – an out-and-back 20K run. It was epic. The heathery lower slopes gradually give way to the kind of arctic tundra that you see on the

Russell and Matthew at the Spittal of Glenshee. Photo: Jamie Smith

tops of the Cairngorms. It is a pleasure to run on this stuff and you can cover the ground quickly. There was a large corrie just beneath the summit which still had a large snow cornice around its upper lip, so we elected to run around the perimeter. We were joined by a Golden Eagle as we made for the summit and, given the conditions, you can imagine we were not disappointed with the view from the top. The main Cairngorm massif, which seemed only a short hop away, looked particularly spectacular. We didn't mess around at the summit. I think we both knew that we still had the guts of this leg still ahead of us. The descent was brisk and pretty straightforward, and we covered the high ground quickly, running most of the way back to the Falls of Tarf. I think we were back there by about 8pm – the sun was starting to set but we still had plenty of daylight ahead. One of the liberating aspects of this kind of running is that conventional routes and paths no longer apply – you can plot the most direct, quickest line and follow it. We had two rivers to ford on our way to the shoulder of Beinn a'Ghlo. We waded across both rivers, which were a bit deeper than we anticipated – up to mid-thigh level, and we were wobbling all over the place on slippery rocks. It was cold and I was aware that a slip and full immersion could have spelt trouble.

The north shoulder of Beinn a'Ghlo is long and steep with no path to follow. This was probably the toughest part of the day and Steve and I were moving in isolation, 20 or 30m apart. Our legs were cold and starting to ache, and we had now been on the go for about three hours, that time at which your body can start to complain and I was aware that the conversation and bonhomie had kind of disappeared. Steve was lagging behind a bit and looked like he was working hard, although he was still moving well. I waited for him, aware of his exertions the previous day, and realising that he might need a bit of encouragement. We stopped to chat and have some grub at about 1000m. Even though it was still relatively light, almost all of the heat had gone from the sun and suddenly we both felt pretty cold. We chucked on leggings, jackets, hats and gloves and agreed that we had to keep moving. It was going to be a clear night and could get very cold, especially at this height. We topped out on the first summit (Carn nan Gabhar, 1121m) at 21:30 and took a few photos. The sun was just dipping below a cloud layer that was forming. We could see layer upon layer of hills and mountains to the south and west. I was amazed at the view to the Lomond Hills in Fife, near to home, and a long way from my current position!

At this height, moving was easy due to the desolate tundra and we headed off for the next Archie, Braigh Coire Chruinn-bhalgain (1070m). As I mentioned earlier, the only true appreciation of the topography of this hill is from the top and it was spectacular, with deep corries hung on either side of the ridge we were running along. We did encounter one slightly tricky, late-season snow cornice that must've been about five metres high, with no obvious way around. It was slightly overhanging and we had to kick holes into it and drag ourselves up and over the top. A slip at this point would have been a major problem. We took the last summit in the late evening and we could now see the flicker of lights in the distance, presumably Blair Atholl, still a fair distance away. There is still a bit of up and down to get off that hill and we were starting to get pretty tired. It was now after 11pm. We finally had mobile reception, and received a text from Steve's wife, Amy, to say that she and the next team would come up to a reservoir on our route down, shaving five or so kilometres off our return leg. We agreed – you'll accept anything at that time of night when you've still got about 15K of running ahead of you!

Our route traversed round the shoulder of Cairn Liath and when we stopped to recce the map I announced to Steve that whilst I was here I was keen to 'bag' that summit too, although only a Munro and not an Archie. He was obviously delighted! It was probably a good plan as we were able to take the path off Cairn Liath, although it's pretty steep and very loose – head torches on, quads complaining vociferously as we descended. The run out was a perfect warm-down over soft, boggy ground and then a mile or so on farm road that was mostly downhill. Then we saw the welcome sight of torchlight in the distance, followed by the voices of Amy and the next team – Mike

Archie's Mountain Challenge added 5 new photos.
June 9, 2015 ·

The sun shone today and yesterday's northern Cairngorms formed a constant beautiful backdrop. These guys on top of glas tuleichan have been following Rabbie in the courier and today they got to meet him.....

+2

👍 Like   💬 Comment   ➤ Share

Donald and David Henderson. I now felt the same mixture of relief and euphoria that Russell and Matthew must have felt about eight hours earlier. Mike and David were itching to go. Beinn Dearg and the sunrise awaited them.

Amy drove us back to the Atholl car park in the Manning camper van. By now I was cooling down a fair bit, and in get-home mode. I stuffed my bike in the car, said my goodbyes and headed off with the heating on, window open and stereo blasting – trying to stay warm and awake. As I headed home I realised how unbelievably hungry I was feeling, and I have never been so happy to encounter a 24-hour McDonald's as I did at Broxden roundabout. I was home and in to bed at about 3:30am, up at seven and back into work for the ward round at 8:30am, grinning from ear to ear. It was great to have made a small contribution to the Challenge and I was desperate to get further involved in the action, which was to happen at the very end of the Challenge, albeit in more typical Scottish weather.

Beinn Dearg night raid
By Mike Donald – with David Henderson

So, I've got a job for you on Tuesday... just need to know if you have your game face on?

This was the thrust of a text I received at work on Monday from good friend and colleague, Russell Duncan, in the knowledge that I had committed to approximately 72 hours availability to assist with the Challenge in whatever shape or form was required.

It was almost midnight when we met Calum and Steve at the end of their enormous and strenuous leg. Earlier I had met David Henderson in the car park by Blair Atholl as arranged. He was almost completely hidden in his vehicle by a raft of outdoor gear, including three sea kayaks and a surf kayak as well as numerous bikes and camping paraphernalia. An instantly likeable chap, I knew that I was going to have a great adventure with Dave. It had been unclear what time we would be setting off but by rough calculations it was very likely that we would be under cover of darkness – which was great, as I had next to no lights with me for the lengthy cycle in to the hill. Not a problem though, as Dave had contingencies for all eventualities and patched over my kit inadequacies with ease. Top man!

We chummed Steve's wife, Amy, up to end of road to save the lads another four kilometres on the road, and it was incredible to watch the head torches bobbing down the hill and towards us at some pace after they had spent many hours moving across poor terrain. Both of them looked like they had seen some action, with wild hair and thousand-yard stares when they arrived. After the briefest of chats, we took charge of Rabbie and cycled back towards the Atholl car park, which was on our route to Beinn Dearg. The cycle up the glen was magical, with herds of deer crossing the track, their eyes reflecting the bike lights as we passed. The night was gin-clear and windless, and both Dave and I could not believe our luck to be out in the wilderness and taking part in this extraordinary Challenge, which we had been following remotely and virtually from the comfort of home up until this point. After ditching the bikes we hiked the remaining few kilometres to the summit of Beinn Dearg and enjoyed an incredible panorama of surrounding peaks as the sun started to rise.

Mike Donald on Beinn Dearg. Photo: David Henderson

A few selfies with Rabbie and a rapid descent back to the bikes was followed by a more rapid and most exhilarating descent (interrupted by a puncture, again saved by Dave, who had a spare pump after my one refused to inflate the tyre). We arrived at the car park at 5am and handed the rabbit on to Amy who set off on her road bike towards Drumochter. I was blown away by Amy's strength on the bike as she powered off up the road with next to no sleep under her belt. My awe was somewhat tempered by the fact that I had to meet her at Drumochter for the next leg, so I stashed the bike in the van and took off after her, determined to get up there in time to boil a few eggs before she arrived – it had become clear that it was not good form for Rabbie to mark time!

DAY 12
10 June 2015
12 ARCHIES

0 10 20 30 40 50 60 70 80 90 100 110 120 130

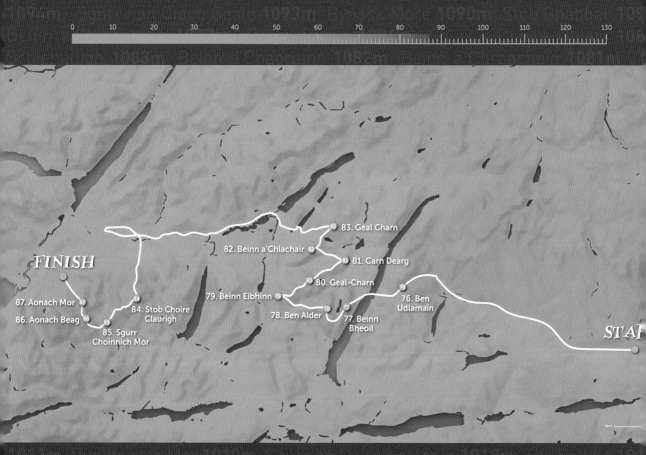

FINISH

83. Geal Charn

82. Beinn a'Chlachair

81. Carn Dearg

80. Geal-Charn

79. Beinn Eibhinn

76. Ben Udlamain

87. Aonach Mor

86. Aonach Beag

84. Stob Choire Claurigh

78. Ben Alder

77. Beinn Bheoil

85. Sgurr Choinnich Mor

STAI

ROAD CYCLE

Blair Atholl to Drumochter: Amy Manning. 30km (450m)

BEN UDLAMAIN

76. Ben Udlamain (1011m): Katie Annan & Mike Donald. 11km (660m)

KAYAK

Kayak across Loch Ericht: David Henderson, Katie Annan, Joe Symonds & Graeme Gatherer. 1.5km

LOCH ERICHT TO LOCH LAGGAN

77. Beinn Bheoil (1019m), 78. Ben Alder (1148m), 79. Beinn Eibhinn (1102m), 80. Geal-Charn (1132m), 81. Carn Dearg (1034m), 82. Beinn a'Chlachair (1087m), 83. Geal Charn (1049m): Joe Symonds & Graeme Gatherer. 37 km (2920m) 2km run out

CYCLE

Loch Laggan to Grey Corries: Tom Fardon & Amy Manning. 32km (260m)

GREY CORRIES TO AONACH MOR

84. Stob Choire Claurigh (1177m), 85. Sgurr Choinnich Mor (1094m), 86. Aonach Beag (1234m), 87. Aonach Mor (1221m): Jason Hardy & Russell Duncan. 23km (2060m)

*Distance in kilometres, (and ascent in metres – this is the cumulative ascent of the leg, even if there is a net descent and the finish is lower than the start). In some cases there was a walk (or run) in or out to the start or finish of a leg without carrying the baton.

Ben Udlamain

By Mike Donald and Kate Annan

Mike: My partner for this next leg over Ben Udlamain was Kate Annan who I knew from work as she was one of our current junior doctors. I had texted her earlier to update her with plans and had received a text back stating:

> I'm in layby 81 – looked like the best one for a kip

If it was not clear already then this message clarified that I was in the company of people who were clearly not quite right in the head, as all this random sleeping in odd places seemed entirely normal to them. Sure enough, I found Katie resting in the boot of her car in layby 81 on the Drumochter Pass at around 05:45 surrounded by artic lorries and truckers doing the same. She seemed completely unperturbed and had had only a few hours' sleep after driving up from Wales overnight, having spent a week climbing in Snowdonia. We boiled up a few eggs and readied our kit for the relatively simple stretch ahead. Amy arrived shortly after, and we headed off with bluebird skies overhead and some cloud inversion to add to one of the most beautiful Scottish mornings I can remember. We set off at a cracking pace – Katie is a little dynamo while I am a lumbering carthorse, and I think she had to stifle a few guffaws at my unorthodox running style, but she was very polite. In fact, I had to tell her to stop calling me 'Dr Donald' and that 'Mike' or 'Hey, you' would be fine. Katie is an experienced mountaineer and responds with Tayside Mountain Rescue Team (and she can also do the box splits and rest her body face down on the ground at the same time) so I knew that I was in safe hands. Approximately 90 minutes later we summitted Beinn Udlamain (1011m) and the scenes were incredible again. Text to Russell from the summit, clearly a bit emotional after zero hours' sleep:

> Summited my friend, the 360 pano is beyond belief. Awe inspiring scenes. I may cry. Hope to be off this bad boy in next 30 mins and hand on to real athletes. M

Crossing Loch Ericht, with the Black Mount (Glencoe) in the distance. Photo: Kate Annan

Katie descended this mountain at an incredible pace and seemed totally without regard for the health of her knees.

Katie: How Mike ran and cycled through the night, then just kept on going for another Archie with a big smile and bucket loads of energy is beyond me. He was also very patient with my obsessive map checking – I guess he understood that I really, really didn't want to go up the wrong hill on my first day! He was an all-round great guy to kick-start my Archies experience with, although we did look like a Shetland pony and a carthorse that had been paired in the traces.

Mike: We could clearly see the power station where David, Graeme and Joe were setting up the kayaks to cross Loch Ericht, and when we eventually arrived at the loch's edge we were greeted with wide smiles and a barely contained energy as they ripped on their dry-suits and spray decks and launched out on to the loch. Katie was also still bubbling with energy and accompanied the lads across the loch. Then she and David each towed a kayak back after dropping off Graeme and Joe, who apparently went off up the mountain like a couple of Alpine goats. I passed out on the boat slip for 20 minutes in the warm sun, and had a surreal moment on waking and wondering where the hell I was – not since University days had I experienced such disorientation on waking in unfamiliar surroundings. David was also somewhat groggy, as he had not slept either since our trip up Beinn Dearg a few hours earlier but was still buzzing and riding the adrenaline wave as he drove us out of Loch Ericht and back towards Drumochter Pass to reunite with our vehicles.

Graeme Gatherer
June 10, 2015

3am breakfast, pre-Archies. Time to rock-n-roll.......

👍 6

👍 Like   ↗ Share

Scorching run over the Ben Alder group
By Graeme Gatherer and Joe Symonds

Graeme: Running the Easains with John Irving, and Chno Dearg with Phil Lacoux in the same day was just for starters! My main course was served up in large portions in a very tasty run from Loch Ericht to Loch Laggan. Our task was to complete the

Ben Alder and Laggan groups which comprised seven Archies, or eight Munros in old money. This time my dining partner was to be Joe Symonds. Joe had been a medical student in Dundee, and a handful of years earlier he had been attached to my GP practice for a few weeks. We had enjoyed a few afternoon runs and bike rides in the local hills and I remembered him as a young, very enthusiastic learner with a great passion for his sport. Our 4am meet-up at the Bridge of Tilt car park confirmed my memory – he was buzzing with enthusiasm and simply raring to go, albeit now with a wee bit of facial hair! Moments later David Henderson and Mike Donald came riding into the car park with beaming smiles and tales of punctures and midnight mountain tops!

Graeme Gatherer and Joe Symonds head off for a big day in the Alder hills. Photo: Kate Annan

Joe Symonds on Beinn Eibhinn, with Ben Alder in the background. Photo: Graeme Gatherer

While Amy cycled up to the Drumochter Pass, David, Joe and I made the long journey up the dirt track from Loch Rannoch to Loch Ericht to await Katie and Mike's arrival from over Ben Udlamain. David, who had been up all night, seemed so much more organised than us and made us cups of tea and fed us in preparation for the day ahead. It certainly wasn't long before Katie and Mike appeared, running swiftly down the heather slopes towards us. Soon we were kayaking almost effortlessly across a near-still Loch Ericht to the foot of Beinn Bheoil. The sky was an endless blue, with warm temperatures forecast, so we planned to travel fast and light carrying minimal kit. David and Katie took some photos and then set about towing the spare kayaks back across the loch. As we made our way up the interminable slopes of Beinn Bheoil (1019m), they slowly disappeared from view and we were then a very lonely pair in a very remote part of the country.

Joe: Continuous Scottish mountain challenges (and there have been quite a few) have always held a fascination for me. In 1990 my father, Hugh Symonds, became the first person to run up, down, and between all the Munros in one continuous effort, taking 66 days. At that time I was six years old, my older brother Andrew was eight, and my younger sister Amy four. Our mother, Pauline, drove us all round in a camper van for three months, supporting and distracting him. It was therefore a great honour for me to be asked to take part in the Archies Mountain Challenge. Likewise for Amy, and her husband Steve, who at the time was working in Ninewells anaesthetic department.

I had informed Russell Duncan, who was strategising for the week, that I would be available on Wednesday June 10th. I clearly hadn't thought this through completely, because I was working in Yorkhill Children's Hospital in Glasgow until midnight on the Tuesday. I got a call from Russell at work at 7pm informing me that I would be required in Blair Atholl at 4am, and that I would be running 25 miles over seven Archies in the Ben Alder region. I managed an hour's sleep at home before setting off at 2am to hook up with the relay. Any tiredness was soon forgotten as I kayaked across Loch Ericht to begin what would be an epic mountain day in perfect conditions with Graeme.

Graeme: Joe is without doubt the most talented runner I know. His road marathon time is nearly world class but it's his mountain running where his strengths lie. As the former British fell running champion and the holder of records across the UK, I knew the run ahead in his company would stretch me to my limits and beyond. We made excellent progress up Beinn Bheoil and Ben Alder (1148m) together but I was operating at an uncomfortable pace throughout. I could feel the 17 miles in my legs from the Sunday and that discomfort never really left me all day. It was a wonderful run however, over some of Scotland's more remote mountains, and a journey rarely taken in entirety. We crossed Beinn Eibhinn (1102m) and Geal-Charn (1132m), using the lingering snowfields to make rapid progress in descent whenever we could, and enjoyed views as far as the eyes could see in every direction. It was a very hot day and even the herds of deer were using the snow to cool down. Drinking from streams and consuming gels on top of every summit, it remained a challenge to stay properly hydrated.

After a long descent into the glen from Carn Dearg (1034m), I was suffering from the heat, the pace and energy levels. I refuelled but it took some 20 minutes to feel strong again. Urging Joe to push on up Beinn a'Chlachair (1087m) which he did at speed, I slowly skirted the hill and then we joined forces again for the seventh Archie of the day – our second Geal Charn (1049m). From our final top we could see our finishing point, and ran at good pace down the fine single-track path through Ardverikie forest and past one of the UK's best known classic rock climbs – Ardverikie Wall. For the second time that day Joe's sister, Amy, this time accompanied by Tom Fardon, cycled off with Rabbie to the next runners. Meanwhile Joe and I congratulated each other on what had been a simply fantastic run, one of the best we'd done! A cold dip in the River Spean was merited, and tales of the day were enjoyed with the others.

Night time decision: The Grey Corries and the Aonachs
By Jason Hardy – with Russell Duncan

It was late afternoon on a beautiful day when Russell and I finally set off up the Grey Corries from Corriechoille farm. Not quite the midday start time we had planned. I'm sure I had mentioned to Russell I needed to be back in Dundee for work at eight the next morning! Were we really aiming to do the Corries, the Aonachs and the Ben this evening? Yeah, no bother! We did have ice axes after all, although they are not the best for running. We made up a little time by setting off up track before Tom and Amy arrived, making them cycle up the track to catch us.

The route we had chosen was through the Lairig, a scramble up Ruigh na Gualainn, then the grassy banks of Beinn Bhan in the blazing early evening sun, to finally top Stob Choire Claurigh (1177m) just after 19:30. We made quick progress along the ridge. At the bealach beyond Sgurr Choinnich Beag we passed a couple of walkers setting up camp for the night. Sensible people.

After Sgurr Choinnich Mor (1094m) we were soon at the crux, and facing an obstacle that had been the subject of more than one discussion in the previous few days. We were at the foot of a steep, wet, grass-strewn, craggy rock face leading to Stob Coire Bhealaich, which although it was more of a scramble than a climb still looked pretty formidable in the fading light. It was getting late. We were still planning to do the Ben, right? Should we go up, or take the considerably longer route round, skirting west below Sgurr a'Bhuic? We went up the direct route. The 'fast' route. How bad could it be? There must be a path somewhere. It is fair to say Russell is not the biggest fan of heights and exposed rock faces. He was enjoying this, though; I could tell. I remember him thanking me for reminding him not to look down as he stood on a rocky ledge, grasping two bits of soggy grass for hand holds: 'Just keep looking up.' I'm sure 'Thank You' was what he said.

We made it to the top physically in one piece, although our nerves might have been in a few more. We were presented with a snow bank to climb for the last 200m of Aonach Beag (1234m). Good job we'd spent the last four hours lugging our ice axes with us. It was pleasant to discover that mountain running shoes have more grip on snow than they do on steep wet grass and rocks. We topped out Aonach Beag at

Russell Duncan on the summit of Aonach Mor. Photo: Jason Hardy

22:30. Thank goodness for the GPS. I am sure there is a lovely cairn at the top, but all we found was a featureless snow-capped expanse. The only thing denoting the summit was a congregation of other walkers' foot prints. The sun was setting and the view stunning. We could even see the Cullin silhouetted by a blood red sky. We reached the top of Aonach Mor (1221m) at 23:00 in the last of the daylight. Decision time.

'Did I mention I have to be in Dundee for 8am, Russell?'

'We're not doing the Ben. It's covered in snow and we're not that well equipped. If it had been evening time then grand, but not in the middle of the night.'

Decision made, we descended to the ski-station car park, Russell making numerous phone calls to keep Rabbie on the move. Running down the snow-filled Goose Gully, I remembered being there only a few months earlier, as I coaxed my son down on a set of skis. I wasn't any quicker in my trainers! Running down the mountain bike route at midnight was fun, and not something I ever expected to do. I even managed to get some air on the drop offs.

We met up with the others in the car park. The indefatigable Amy Manning cycled Rabbie round to Glen Nevis for a brief period of rest. I think someone must have driven me back to my car at Moy. I really can't remember. I do, however, know I made it back to Dundee, and I think I even managed a shower and a change of clothes. Work colleagues might claim otherwise.

DAY 13
11 June 2015
13 ARCHIES

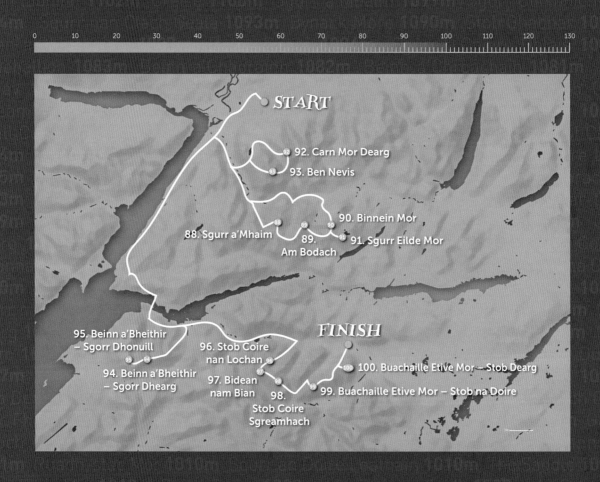

START

92. Carn Mor Dearg

93. Ben Nevis

90. Binnein Mor

88. Sgurr a'Mhaim

89. Am Bodach

91. Sgurr Eilde Mor

95. Beinn a'Bheithir – Sgorr Dhonuill

96. Stob Coire nan Lochan

FINISH

100. Buachaille Etive Mor – Stob Dearg

94. Beinn a'Bheithir – Sgorr Dhearg

97. Bidean nam Bian

98. Stob Coire Sgreamhach

99. Buachaille Etive Mor – Stob na Doire

ROAD CYCLE

Cycle link to Mamores: Amy Manning. 17km (200m)

MAMORES

88. Sgurr a'Mhaim (1099m), 89. Am Bodach (1032m), 90. Binnein Mor (1130m), 91. Sgurr Eilde Mor (1010m): Kate Annan & Brian Stevenson. 24km (2330m)

ROAD CYCLE

Cycle link, head of Glen Nevis down to Youth Hostel: Amy Manning & Tom Fardon. 7km (90m)

CMD & THE BEN

92. Carn Mor Dearg (1220m), 93. Ben Nevis (1345m): Nicky Conway & Paul Fettes. 16km (1590m)

CYCLE LINK

Glen Nevis to Ballachulish: Amy Manning. 29km (450m)

BALLACHULISH HORSESHOE

94. Beinn a'Bheithir – Sgorr Dhearg (1024m), 95. Beinn a'Bheithir – Sgorr Dhonuill (1001m): Steve Manning & Tom Fardon. 13km (1350m)

ROAD CYCLE

Cycle link to Bidean, Glencoe: Gary Tompsett. 11km (260m)

BIDEAN TRIO

96. Stob Coire nan Lochan (1115m), 97. Bidean nam Bian (1150m), 98. Stob Coire Sgreamhach (1072m): Simon Crawley & Andrew Dalton. 9km (1210m)

BUACHAILLE ETIVE MOR

99. Stob na Doire (1011m), 100. Stob Dearg (1022m): Russell Duncan & Mike Donald. 9km (1130m)

*Distance in kilometres, (and ascent in metres – this is the cumulative ascent of the leg, even if there is a net descent and the finish is lower than the start). In some cases there was a walk (or run) in or out to the start or finish of a leg without carrying the baton.

Mamores Initiation, for Brian Stevenson
By Kate Annan

At some hour in the night my phone startled me awake in an unfamiliar van somewhere in Glen Nevis. Russell was calling to say that the Carn Mor Dearg arête in the dark was looking like a no-go for him and Jay that night, so they were heading down after Aonach Mor. With something as exciting and consuming as the Archies Mountain Challenge, it can be hard to resist pushing on, especially when you know the outside world is watching and the clock is ticking. Several people had had to make a safe decision when there was a great temptation to give in to summit fever. I teased him that this would go down on his record as calling mountain rescue, and wished him and Jay a speedy descent. Then I turned my attention to the man loitering nearby; something about him made me suspect that this might be my running partner for the morning – Brian.

We set off along the Glen Nevis road together a few hours later. Brian is an experienced runner, but I learnt later that he had never climbed a Munro before; the four Archies in the Mamores is certainly not a bad way to start! I picked our route to take us up a good path for the first few kilometres, then steeply up the side of Sgurr a'Mhaim (1099m), avoiding the scree until the last few metres. We did avoid the scree, but it was a murderously steep slope that had us on all fours. Brian took to the steep terrain like a newborn goat and didn't voice any of the curses that I'm sure he had for me and for Russell, his good friend who had convinced him to join in this wonderfully mental Challenge. We summitted a little too late to see the sun rise, but what a view to summit to. The cloud inversion stayed with us for most of our trip along the ridge, clearing in time for us to descend back into Glen Nevis.

I had thought that we might be able to skirt around the tops on the ridge that didn't make Archie status. The first attempt at doing so resulted in backing out of taking a non-climber on a traverse of a cliff without any gear or rope; the second with a panic that I had lost Brian when we somehow went opposite sides of a short prominence. From then on we mainly followed the ridge as it came. One more attempt to avoid a climb led us to a big sugar bowl. The best escape point was pretty much at the top that we'd been trying to avoid – another absolute failure to save time and energy from me.

Kate Annan in Glen Nevis, after a Mamore morning. Photo: Brian Stevenson

Am Bodach (1032m) was followed by Binnein Mor (1130m), from the top of which was a steep descent, with no way to avoid the snow, before another steep climb up Sgurr Eilde Mor (1010m). I had an axe with me, but decided that using it to descend would probably scare my axeless, mountain-virgin comrade; and giving the axe to him would probably have been even worse. As our patch of steep snow ended abruptly on steep scree we had to adopt a more measured approach than seems to have been favoured during the Challenge, but we made it with no injuries and with dry backsides. At the summit of our fourth and final Archie of the day we struggled to smile for the summit selfie, but behind our grimaces we were both absolutely enthralled by the incredible views we had been running (and staggering) through. A message from base camp came in on that top:

Temperature inversion on the Mamores, with Schiehallion on the horizon. Photo: Brian Stevenson

> Great lines guys you are going really well. Bravo, bravo, bravo, bravo, bravissimo...

What a fantastic boost to morale to know that people were keeping an eye on us, and that we weren't going as slowly as it was feeling at that point. We looked west along the ridge again with refreshed eyes and really saw what we'd achieved.

Another steep descent took us down into Glen Nevis. Much of the way back to Steall Meadows the 'path' is really just a popular route through the mud. It was soft under tired feet, and not the effortless running we were wishing for after over two kilometres of ascent, and all the downhill that comes with it. It was on the meadow that we came across other people for the first time. They were clearly very confused to see us – I suppose where we had come from must have been a complete mystery, as they had been camping up the glen and it was still morning. The mighty Falls of Steall prompted a quick celebratory cartwheel for Rabbie, then it was a final blast down the track to where Amy and Tom were waiting. I remember a tip I was given on my first ever hill running descent: 'the trick is to feel like you're flying... but don't actually go flying.' It was a close one for me. Time to belatedly celebrate Brian's Munro (and Archie) initiation with rhubarb gin and whisky, then tuck into porridge and coffee with the late-risers of the world – do they even know what they're missing?

We had just enough time for a swim in the river while Paul and Nicky ran to the top of the UK and back. Quick congratulations, then onwards to Glencoe for more planning and a proper meal not cooked on a camp stove, with the tracker being compulsively refreshed on a gaggle of gadgets. I had been impressed by the fitness, stamina and positivity of all the people around me, but the feat of planning was something else.

Bike link
By Tom Fardon – with Amy Manning

It was early, but we weren't up as early as Brian and Titch (Katie), who had set off at first light to chase around Brian's first Archies, and indeed, his first go at hill running. Amy and I set off up the Glen Nevis road on our bikes to meet them off the mountain. We didn't wait long to find them bombing down the path. A quick handover, and we were back down the glen to hand over to Rear Admiral Fettes and Nicky Conway who were champing at the bit to get up the Ben. As is typical of a Scottish summer, they set off in shorts and short sleeves, with ice axes and crampons attached to their rucksacks.

A new kind of CMD, and the Ben
By Nicky Conway – with Paul Fettes

Prior to joining the Challenge I, like many others, had been following the progress of Rabbie via the live GPS tracker. Until this point, progress had been slow owing to adverse weather conditions and so it was difficult to envisage which hills were on my itinerary for the four days that I had committed to the Challenge. On day one of duty, I woke at four in the morning, sun already high in the sky, and headed in my car in a northwesterly direction in the hope that further instruction would follow. Halfway up the A9, Paul's text directed me to Glen Nevis at which point I started to get excited, albeit a bit nervous, at the mention of the need for ice axes.

Working on the false impression that the team were waiting for me, the drive went quickly. I grabbed a quick breakfast in Fort William prior to entering the glen, followed by a hurried change into my running kit before meeting my fellow runners and then... we waited. Rabbie was apparently halfway round the Ring of Steall and wasn't due back for a couple of hours. I had a coffee and sat with the others in the sun.

My wait was rewarded as I was chosen, alongside Paul, to take Rabbie to the highest point in the UK. It's estimated that over 100,000 people climb the Ben every year. To my shame, that figure did not include me prior to this Challenge (although I've got vague memories of an aborted attempt as a moaning child on a long hot day with my increasingly frustrated parents). The chosen route was to summit via Carn Mor Dearg (CMD) and the arête that joins this to Ben Nevis's east side.

Paul is an experienced hill runner and so I was somewhat surprised at the sedate pace at which we set out. It became clear fairly early on that this was the pace that was to be maintained regardless of gradient and it wasn't long before I was at my threshold. The traverse to the CIC Memorial Hut provided some respite, before a straight ascent of CMD. The ultimate humiliation was soon to follow, as Paul offered to take my rucksack in order to speed things up. This was followed soon after by some tentative enquiries regarding my ability to traverse ridges and my confidence in descending. I was feeling dizzy. Paul was getting worried.

In our family, 'CMD' is an abbreviation for 'chronic mild disappointment', a phrase coined by close friends experiencing a fairly tough few years of bringing up three young children. My childhood experience of trying to walk up the Ben would be a good example of this form of CMD, meted out to over-ambitious parents. It's fair to say the views from atop the CMD were the antithesis of the Conway family CMD. The Ben loomed into view to the west, its north-east gullies still snow-filled, as was the shoulder that was to take us to the summit. The distant climbers on the snowfield provided some much needed perspective. Fort William was well below us to the north-west, whilst the rest of our panorama was taken up by mountain after mountain after mountain.

After a quick photo stop and a bite to eat, I was back in the room. The schist of the arête was a joy to scramble across and we were soon on the shoulder. The warm sun had softened the snow, making easy climbing to the summit. Summer prevailed as we continued in shorts and T-shirts with ice axes remaining on our backs – the coruscating light dazzling in its intensity. We passed a few bemused climbers before experiencing the odd sensation of suddenly finding ourselves within a large crowd in the middle of nowhere as we reached the top.

Ben Nevis from Carn Mor Dearg. Photo: Nicky Conway

The spring snow enabled a rapid descent down the western slopes, at the expense of all feeling below the knee and a few untimely plunges into unseen burns. We continued, past droves of walkers, under the watchful eye of the Archie team waiting in the glen below. Soon after, Rabbie was successfully handed over to Amy Manning, waiting on her bike to transport him to Ballachulish. After a quick cool down in the River Nevis I sat down in the shade to rehydrate, left with a strange feeling of pride to have been able to contribute; privilege to have been allowed to do so in such an iconic setting; and awe at what was becoming clear to me was such a huge logistical undertaking. I waited for my next assignment.

A Canter over the Ballachulish Horseshoe
By Tom Fardon – with Steve Manning

From Glen Nevis, Amy took Rabbie and set off to cycle to Ballachulish, where she would hand over to husband Steve, and me. After a few minutes enjoying good company in the warm sunshine, we suddenly realised that we needed to beat her to Ballachulish, so we set off to the meeting point. We only just beat her there – so a dash up to the school gates was met with a 'Where have you been?' look, and we were off.

On paper, the Ballachulish horseshoe pair of Archies are both low mountains, only just Archies in fact. What I failed to grasp before we set off was that the start of the run was essentially at sea level. So began a constant climb of the best part of 1000m, in a straight line, up the southern ridge of Sgorr Dhearg. Steve is a quick lad. I was a wheezy old man, hanging on for dear life behind him. The terrain was completely different from the Cairngorm climbs – rather than long domed summits, with wide approaches, the western mountains are steep, the paths are narrow, the ridges drop off precipitously on both sides. Frankly, it gave me the Willies. Running up the ridge with only four feet of path to separate me from a long drop, Steve was a fantastic guide: 'Just look straight ahead on this bit, Tom; probably best not to look to the right...'

But what a view from the top! Where there had been cloud, snow, rain, drizzle, and an urge to get off the summits in the Cairngorms, the summit of Sgorr Dhearg (1024m) offered us a 360-degree view of Scotland. The Ben, the Cairngorms, the Cullin Ridge, the isle of Jura. A phenomenal sight. It has to be my favourite Archie summit photo from the week. But we didn't hang around too long as we were off down the saddle to start the second climb. This was even more technical, with some scrambling up rocks, and some very narrow paths. More looking straight ahead, and not looking right, and we were on the top of Sgorr Dhonuill (1001m), job done.

Mountain man Gary Tompsett had passed on some advice about the return leg. Unfortunately he passed it on through an intermediary. The message started off as 'Have a look at the western slope, and see if you can contour back along; it could save you some time on the return leg.' This became, 'Descend to 700m, and you'll be able to save loads of time contouring round to the start point.' 700m turned out to be a large rock field. And once we were into it, we had crossed the Rubicon, and were committed to it.

Tom Fardon on Sgurr Dearg. Photo: Tom Fardon

My mountain goat abilities are not renowned, and my choice of footwear wasn't exactly tailored to traversing a 60-degree slope of rough scree. But we made it through, and decided on 'the direct route' down, at full whack. Steve was a true gentleman again – every time he started pulling away from me on the descent, he'd very thoughtfully fall over, allowing me to catch up.

Gary and Amy were waiting by the gate at the bottom of the path, ready to take Rabbie on to Glen Coe. And then it was over. Amy and Steve left to get to Glasgow, and I returned to my car in an otherwise empty car park. Everyone else had moved on to Glen Coe, and more adventures. It was only when I got to the car that I realised I probably needed a new pair of running shoes.

I was left with a three-hour drive back to Dundee, and a lot to reflect on. Five days, 86km on foot with over 4000m climbing, 10 Archie summits, 120km cycled, two bags of peanut M&Ms, two full Scottish breakfasts, a curry, too many bottles of juice, probably not enough water, too many energy gels, and far too little sleep. But what an experience. What a thing to be part of.

A good day off work: Bidean trio
By Andrew Dalton – with Simon Crawley

Having dragged ourselves out of bed at some unearthly hour in the morning so that we could be in Glen Coe by 8am, ready to tackle the Ballachulish Horshoe, Simon and I were sent word that the schedule had slipped. We were now to head to Glen Nevis at a more leisurely pace. I stole a welcome extra hour in bed before Simon arrived, and off we set. When we arrived everyone was in great spirits recounting the adventures of the preceding days. At that point Rabbie was somewhere in the Mamore mountains, and there was plenty of time to plan the day. It was suggested that it might be better for the rather 'broken' Tom Fardon and Steve Manning to do the Ballachulish Horseshoe, and to leave Simon and my fresh legs for the longer outing over Bidean nam Bian and the two adjacent Archies later in the day. (Which left Simon making an apologetic call to his wife – her evening plans would have to be cancelled as he wouldn't now be back to look after the children!)

The rest of the morning and afternoon was spent engrossed in stories of the trip to-date while sitting in the sun surrounded by fantastic scenery. Just being there meant that we had a great day, even before we got involved in the action.

So this is how we found ourselves in a Pass of Glencoe car park, about to head into the hills at 8:30pm for what was my first active part in the Challenge. The sky was still blue, the sun was shining, and we knew we were in for some spectacular evening climbing and views.

Simon evidently felt he wanted to see these views as quickly as possible, as he set off like a greyhound released from its traps. Thankfully he reined it in slightly and we progressed at a more manageable pace up our first Archie of the night – Stob Coire nan Lochan (1115m) which for some strange reason is not a Munro. As we scrambled our way to the summit, the views that we were afforded by the clear sky and still-shining sun were quite incredible – made better by the fact that were it not for the Archie Challenge there is no way on a Thursday evening we would be up there to experience it.

From Stob Coire nan Lochan we then headed for the ridge connecting us to our second Archie, Bidean nam Bian (1150m). Thankfully, this intimidating looking ridge was fairly straightforward, with only very sparse sprinklings of snow interrupting our rocky terrain. Bidean is the highest mountain in Argyll, and from the summit we savoured a full panoramic view, from Schiehallion to the east, Ben Cruachan nestling behind Loch Etive to the south-west, and to the vast white hulk of Ben Nevis looming over the menacing black ridge of the Aonach Eagach in the north-east – fantastic!

From here, we had one more Archie to bag before descending to hand over – Stob Coire Sgreamhach (1072m). The sun was now setting, and after a quick check of the map Simon took this as his cue to speed up again to try and ensure he got back to the car in daylight. After summitting Sgreamhach we descended quickly to the pre-arranged rendezvous point where Russell and Mike would be awaiting our arrival. We found a reasonable route off the ridge (lots of snow remained on this side which we were trying to avoid if possible), and then jogged down towards the welcome silhouettes in the distance.

After a brief chat, we watched Mike and Russell head off into the night, before walking back out to the car. We left Glen Coe at 11:30pm, after what had been a fantastic day, but we both had to return home and work the next day. We were sad to be leaving the Challenge, especially because we knew that it would be finished before either of us would be available again. The journey home was very quick – or at least it was for me, as sleeping has that effect on your time perception... Thanks, Simon!

Twin Peaks on the Great Shepherd of Etive
By Mike Donald – with Russell Duncan

> Bring your legs, reckon you and I are on late shift again. The Buchaille.

Nice one! My favourite mountain, and with Russell – what could be better?

After Beinn Udlamain, I had enjoyed a decent lamb Kashmiri in Dalwhinnie, and a bit of Archie 'down time' with a kip in the sun by Loch Laggan. I then gave runners Joe Symonds and Graeme Gatherer a lift back to their cars in Blair Atholl, after which I decided to head home for the night. The next day it was a stunning drive up from Dundee to Glen Coe. I will never tire of that view when you come over Rannoch

Moor, look west and the Great Herdsman (or Shepherd) of Etive looms up in front of you. It seemed a bit surreal to think that I would be on top of that behemoth in a few hours' time. Finally, after incredible efforts from all the teams that day, Russell and I left to pick up Rabbie from Simon Crawley and Andrew Dalton who had taken on Bidean nam Bian. We arrived at the pre-designated cairn around 10pm and could just make out figures on the ridge. Simon and Andrew launched themselves down a snow cornice, which looked pretty airy from where I was standing, and within 30 minutes they were standing next to us. We took off at pace, full of catecholamines that had been building up during the day. Russell had covered in excess of 100km in the previous few days with goodness knows how many metres of ascent, but he still drove us forward. We performed a pretty sketchy dance around a couple of crags, then enjoyed a good run up to a bealach before we ascended Stob na Doire (1011m) the first Archie on the Buachaille complex. A genius bit of navigation from Russell saw us knock off a fair bit to intersect with a path which headed upwards into the dark. We took it in turns to set pace over the ridge until we reached the get out point, which had looked a bit touch-and-go from bottom of hill. We shone our head torches over the edge of the cornice and reassured each other (without much conviction) that it looked 'fine'. All I could see was a dark abyss and the headlights of cars way below. We summitted Stob Dearg (1022m) shortly after 1am and disturbed a chap who was spending the night sleeping on top of the hill. We had a good laugh with him after we recovered from the fright of almost standing on him in the dark. We descended quickly and cut a few snow steps in to the cornice as we dropped off the ridge. It was a huge relief to be past the crux, and we enjoyed a good run off the hill, swapping tales and talking, before reaching Gary Tompsett and Tim Gomersall who were champing at the bit for their night run. Rabbie was handed over to Katy Boocock who cycled the short way up to the Glencoe Resort car park before unleashing Gary and Tim up the Black Mount. Russell and I parted company with plans to head east and sleep in our own beds. I arrived home at 4:30am to snatch a couple of hours' sleep before the household awakened and normal service resumed.

What a privilege it was to exist within the Archie bubble, albeit only for a few days. I met some incredible people and am in awe of the vision and logistical management required to pull something like this off. A total reinforcement that life is about experiences and not about having more 'stuff'. We are blessed to live in such an extraordinary country and also to work with and associate with some truly unique individuals.

Archie's Mountain Challenge added 8 new photos —
with **Tom Fardon** and 2 others.
June 12, 2015 · €

So its time for report of the last 24 hours. I don't think Rabbie (or is he Harry the hare now) has been to bed for a couple of days as we sought to maximise the good weather, near 24 hours light and influx of fresh legs. Brian Stevenson and Kate Annan took off up the Mamores on Thursday morning at 0300 - Brian on his first ever mountains ably shepherded by his Mountain Rescue partner Kate. They handed over to Paul and Nicky who tackled The Ben and Carn Mor Dearg in just under 4 hours with their fresh legs - great effort lads. During this time the wearied field team from the previous 72 hours took some well deserved R&R and a wash in the River Nevis. Then the glencoe relay commenced - Tom and Steve first on the Ballachulish Horseshoe, Simon Crawley and Andrew Dalton on Bidean Nam Bian then myself and Mike Donald on Buachaille Etive Mor, the Great Shepherd of Glen Etive. Despite summiting the second Archie on this at about 1am we hadn't needed head torches and there was a dude sleeping up there! I don't know who was more surprised to see someone else. We handed over to Katie Boocock who cycled to the Ski centre where Gary Tompsett and Tim Gomersall were waiting like greyhounds in the traps after watching the challenge unfold over the last 2 weeks. Since then Rabbie has been down the Etive mountains where he was reaquainted with Brian and "Titch" - his personal mountain guide to go over Ben Starav. At the foot of Ben Starav was David Henderson waiting in his trusty kayak to paddle Rabbie down Loch Etive to Taynuilt. No doubt exhausted Rabbie is at this moment half way up Ben Crauchan.

Each of these sections has been linked by Amy Manning who has been ready and willing to ship Rabbie by bike to the next mountain whenever this has been required - she has been a real star of the show.

I hope this gives you some idea of what its been like for Rabbie and his porters since last saturday.

I can't express how impressed and humbled I have been while in the company of all of these fine people who have volunteered their time for this monumental effort and those who have supported them from home to allow this to happen. It has been fun, but very hard going.

So the challenge continues and Rabbie moves on, another 24 to go I think after Ben Cruachan.

Go on then share this post and - please consider donating to this historic challenge and worthy cause.

Text TCHA15 followed by the amount you would like to donate to 70070 or visit Archies Mountain Challenge page on www.justgiving.com

👍 Like   💬 Comment   ➤ Share

DAY 14
12 June 2015
10 ARCHIES

START

102. Creise

101. Meall a'Bhuirdh

103. Stob Ghabhar

110. Beinn a'Chreachain

FINISH

104. Stob Coir'an Albannaich

105. Ben Starav

108. Beinn an Dothaidh

109. Beinn Achaladair

107. Ben Dorain

106. Ben Cruachan

ROAD CYCLE

Cycle link to Glencoe Ski Centre: Katy Boocock. 7km (120m)

GLENCOE TO ETIVE

101. Meall a'Bhuirdh (1108m), 102. Creise (1100m), 103. Stob Ghabhar (1090m), 104. Stob Coir'an Albannaich (1044m): Tim Gomersall & Gary Tompsett. 23km (2070m), 3km run out.

BEN STARAV

105. Ben Starav (1078m): Katie Annan & Brian Stevenson. 6km (890m) and 600m kayak tow in Loch Etive. 3km walk in and 4km run out.

KAYAK TO TAYNUILT

David Henderson & Gordon Wishart (Katie Sims also accompanied David and Gordon for part of the way down the loch). 14km.

ROAD CYCLE

Cycle to Cruachan: Paul Fettes. 11km (200m)

BEN CRUACHAN

106. Ben Cruachan (1126m): Jason Hardy & Giles Ruck. 11km (1090m)

ROAD CYCLE

Cycle from Loch Awe to Bridge of Orchy: Brian Stevenson. 31km (420m)

BRIDGE OF ORCHY TO LOCH LYON

107. Ben Dorain (1076m), 108. Beinn an Dothaidh (1004m), 109. Beinn Achaladair (1038m), 110. Beinn a'Chreachain (1081m): Nicky Conway & Katy Boocock. 26km (2010m)

ROAD CYCLE

Glen Lyon road cycle to Camusvrachan: Paul Fettes. 20km (200m), and 7km back to campsite.

*Distance in kilometres, (and ascent in metres – this is the cumulative ascent of the leg, even if there is a net descent and the finish is lower than the start). In some cases there was a walk (or run) in or out to the start or finish of a leg without carrying the baton.

Sunrise over the Black Mount

By Gary Tompsett – with Tim Gomersall

I was deep in a busy sports event management summer. Hopefully woven within this would be an opportunity to pounce on a section of the Challenge that was not too far from Glasgow. Having helped in some of the initial planning, I watched the tracking (didn't we all?), trying to predict the team's schedule, poised and ready for action. The chance came, Glen Coe was the news – an area I know well. Glen Coe would become Black Mount, which was less familiar territory. Despite suspecting that the schedule would slip again, I decided to head up early to meet some members of the Challenge team. So, a few hours later it was a pleasure to hang out with them outside the Glencoe Inn (The Gathering), enjoying good food and coffee in fine weather. I was able to put faces to the valiant heroes seen on social media, grainy images and tracking dots of the previous week or so. I was also able to experience the 'thrill of the wait' as the baton approached, and partake in a little route planning, imparting some of my knowledge of the area. I even managed to cycle Rabbie from Ballachulish village into Glen Coe for the Bidean leg, having brought a bike just in case.

Fast forward a few hours, by which time darkness had fallen. My rumoured stage partner had arrived, in the form of a wild-haired Tim Gomersall, in his student-jumble of a car, but with a relaxed air that suggested that the upcoming mission was right up his street. (In fact, Tim had a pedigree that consumed severe mountain escapades – and normally before breakfast, which was handy, as we weren't about to get sleep on this night.) Katy Boocock waited with us at the foot of Buachaille Etive Mor as we packed for our stage. She had been given the unenviable task of cycling from there along the A82 to the Glencoe ski resort, in the dark. But it was now about 1am, and at least the road was quiet. We had discussed whether to take ice axes (but not crampons) though it was clear that the snow would be soft. At my shameful suggestion, and Tim's disdain, we took axes. We stared impatiently at the dark hulk of Stob Dearg, waiting to see torches. Come on! Then tiny spots of light appeared, and soon runners Russell and Mike arrived. Katy cycled off, and Tim and I drove to the car park at the resort. All was well, and we were like coiled springs!

As Katy arrived at the car park, we took the baton and started our ascent at about 2am. Lungs filled with crisp mountain air, and we dug in for the stiff ascent on a beautifully clear and still night. I had not been on these hills before, but it didn't matter. Tim and I would be on our A-game for navigation, regardless of the weather. We ascended into stunning mountains, wriggling between the eerie out-of-season structures of the ski lifts. We ran joyously over the high ground, as the sun infiltrated as a glow and then rose in full glory. We passed by big crumbling cornices, crossed sweet snow banks and skipped gazelle-like through mountainous rock fields, chatting as we flew. Keeping in touch with the detail of the map to optimise our route, we pushed hard, hands on knees, as we ascended mountain after mountain, and I endeavoured to match Tim's youthful pace. We descended scree-littered paths, spitting rocks, grabbing snacks, but never stopping. This was how to run mountains! All was good.

As for the mountain sequence, it was obvious, as long as we did not forget an early dog-leg: Meall a'Bhuiridh (1108m), Creise (1100m), Clach Leathad (1099m), an awkward saddle transition to Stob Ghabhar (1090m), then a summit-shaving long-leg to Stob Coir' an Albannaich (1044m), before dropping towards Loch Etive, and our handover to the mighty atom Kate Annan, and her running partner, Brian Stevenson. We straight-lined this descent. Research indicated that we should have picked up a path in the corrie by the Allt Mheuran. Instead we were on some very rough steep ground. Tim actually slowed and I knew that we would finish as equals!

The most complex, potentially embarrassing part was yet to come, though. We had agreed to meet the next team at a track junction at 200 metres, but there was an early morning temperature inversion, with the lower 250 metres swathed in cloud. It was stunning, but somewhat a hindrance to meeting anyone. There was no phone signal. We were also behind schedule, having set off considerably later than expected. As we neared the area, I decided an old fashioned method was required. Stop, stand still, listen, call out loudly and clearly, 'Hellooooo...' Stand still, listen. Although we didn't hear back, they had heard us. We descended, and we met. Leg accomplished. As they headed off up Ben Starav, we ambled down, collected their car, and drove through Glen Etive (meeting someone running with her dog up the Etive road, who I knew of course!) back to our cars. Tim and I had enjoyed a perfect day (at night). I have since followed Tim's exploits. Amongst many juicy ideas and exploits, he went on to destroy the record for the Cuillin Ridge traverse in winter with Finlay Wild. For this, he did need to use an axe!

Ben Starav and a quick dip

By Kate Annan – with Brian Stevenson

After a series of awe-inspiring runs through the night, Brian and I were positioned at the 200 metre contour on the shoulder of Ben Starav ready to receive the baton at 07:00. A misjudged patch of mud had already seen me sink up to my knees that morning; thankfully I had not yet taught Brian that the correct mountain etiquette at such a time is to control your laughter just long enough to take photographic evidence, then proceed to collapse into a heap of mockery, so I was promptly retrieved from the bog. We watched a shroud of haar rush in to envelop Glen Etive then cover us on our vantage point; only the shouts through the mists alerted us to Gary and Tim's approach for handover.

It was time to take Rabbie on another adventure, up through the last tendrils of the haze, then out and into the splendour of the top of Ben Starav (1078m). Yet another day of 360-degree views to savour, with a pathless descent down to our next handover point on the shores of Loch Etive. By that time the sun was beating down and there were no questions – we were going in the loch, and taking Rabbie with us. Soon he was off again, spirited away by the sea kayakers towards Taynuilt and Ben Cruachan. The day wasn't over for Brian, who had a cycle leg to catch; but it was time for me to take a step back from the Challenge, and realise just how much I would miss it.

Kate Annan and Rabbie in Loch Etive. Photo: Katie Sims

Glen Etive Paddle
By David Henderson – with Gordon Wishart & Katie Sims

The sun warmed us, and Loch Etive glistened as we made out the dots descending rapidly towards us while we waited on the south shore of the loch, beneath Starav. They were shifting across rutted, tussocky ground like mountain hares! It was now getting very warm and we even felt the need to remove our kayak cags.

With a few whoops and shrieks Kate was in the loch and going for the first swim leg on the Challenge! Gordon and I just looked at each other; one word – Baltic! Quickly he paddled beside Kate, with Katie Sims doing the photo shoot. Brian had no option but to follow. He was up for a swim tow across on the back of my kayak. At this point we were a little concerned, as Loch Etive is cold higher up, even though it is a sea loch. Suddenly after 50-100m Kate was rolling on to the back deck of Gordon's kayak with ease. She had clearly done this before and was now completely out of the water... whereas Brian hasn't! He is a tall lad and after several goes at doing the 'spatchcock chicken' manoeuvre we decided just to do what worked, with him being pulled behind.

You cool down pretty quickly in water like this. Brian was doing brilliantly hanging on the back of the kayak, even though most of him was in the water. Well, we just needed to paddle harder and faster as Brian was getting a bit of cramp with the cold shock. Once we reached the other side we could relax and speed Archie the 16K onwards to Taynuilt jetty.

Kate Annan hitching a lift with Gordon Wishart. Photo: Katie Sims

After around 20 minutes of paddling the still loch turned choppy due to the headwind from the west. Great, a Force 4 wind on the nose after the pond-like start! With clear blue skies it was such a good day for the hills. We pressed on to rendezvous with Jay and Paul after a brief interlude to let Katie land and rest 4K from Taynuilt. Gordon and I then just focused on matching each other's stroke before he pulled his 'Senna' move 100m from Taynuilt! Archie was safely handed over to Paul after another water journey and then piloted on his way up towards Cruachan for the afternoon.

It was such a privilege to be involved in the AMC with kindred spirits, and to witness the effort and achievement displayed by all was humbling. For me it is only once you look back on these events and experiences that you really appreciate the value and the effort everyone involved put in to this fantastic event. Thank you Paul and team for your management and logistical support in putting this together and succeeding.

The paddlers set off down Loch Etive. Ben Cruachan is in the background. Photo: Kate Annan

Ben Cruachan
By Jason Hardy – with Giles Ruck

I was relaxing back in Dundee. Having finished what I thought was my last stint of the Challenge I could get back to my new favourite hobby: tracker watching. The team looked to be making good progress.

19:18 pm. Text from Russell:

> Mate, Archie calls. Ben Cruachan needs done tomorrow. Easy 10km up and down Big path. Could be as early as 9am but you know how these things slide

Arse. Had I really said I was available? Early start, then...

Having checked the tracker in the morning, a 9am start looked optimistic. I drove to the jetty at Taynuilt where I was joined by Nicky Conway, Katy Boocock and Paul Fettes. We waited for a while in glorious sunshine, looking up Loch Etive to await the arrival of the kayakers. Paul was ready to cycle up the road to the visitor centre for the Cruachan Power Station. Nicky and Katy didn't really need to be there because they wouldn't be needed until later in the day, but these relaxed moments of contemplation were some of the best moments of the Challenge. It was good to spend time with other like-minded individuals, and involvement in this event was proving strangely addictive. After a while, paddlers Dave Henderson and Gordon Wishart appeared on the glassy water and we watched them slowly approach, their paddles dipping into the water with metronomic regularity. Once they had handed Rabbie over to Paul, I drove up to the visitor centre to meet my running partner for the day, Giles Ruck.

The sun shone. It was not long until Paul appeared, grinning from ear to ear. Giles and I duly set off just after midday, and made quick progress up to and around the reservoir, then sharply up to the summit of Ben Cruachan (1126m). Not much time for hanging about, a few quick photos, and back down to the visitor centre to pass Rabbie on to waiting cyclist Brian Stevenson.

Easy 10km up and down. Yes. Big path. Yes. 9am start. I don't think so.

Time enough left in the day to enjoy a drink in the sunshine and realise this was definitely my last Archie of the Challenge.

Bridge of Orchy to Glen Lyon
By Nicky Conway – with Katy Boocock

It would be tempting to infer when reading these accounts that the Archie Challenge was one mad dash across the Scottish Highlands and that all those involved were living off coffee and energy gels for the duration. Whilst I would agree with the former, the complexity of shepherding so many willing volunteers into the correct place at the correct time resulted in a lot of sitting about. And very pleasant it was too. Since completing my first leg at 11am on the Thursday, I had had dinner in Glencoe village; camped at Rannoch Moor; had a picnic whilst waiting on a kayak on the banks of Loch Etive; sunbathed at the bottom of Ben Cruachan; driven to drop off cars at Glen Lyon; and returned to Bridge of Orchy. It's worth noting that for Paul, this was a fairly typical day for the entire two-week duration of the Challenge.

It was now 5pm on the Friday and I was itching to get going. This leg would be my second and final contribution to the Challenge and one that would take me from the heat of the day on the edge of Rannoch Moor to leafy Glen Lyon in the falling dusk. My fellow-runner was Katy Boocock who I had met the previous evening in Glencoe. She was one of an army of like-minded folk that were seemingly able to drop everything at the mention of running up a hill in the dark. It turns out that Paul knows quite a few of these people.

Brian Stevenson passed Rabbie over to us in Bridge of Orchy having cycled up Glen Orchy from the foot of Ben Cruachan. From there, a steady ascent allowed us to gain the col between Beinn Dorain (1076m) and Beinn an Dothaidh (1004m). Katy's pace was a welcome relief from the rather more intense session up the Ben the previous day. With the excellent visibility, our route to Glen Lyon was obvious. The curved summit plateaus were lacking in drama but were a welcome reminder of the topography that I associate with home. We shared backstories and discovered mutual acquaintances and interests before progressing on to the more meaty topics of family, politics and even religion! As the sun dropped in the sky and the light adopted warmer tones, we notched up some easy miles on the plateau, and over Beinn Achaladair (1038m) and Beinn a'Chreachain (1081m). I was in a reflective mood as my attention shifted between the sun setting over the very hills that Rabbie had recently scaled in the north-west and my lengthening shadow that ran beside me on my right, over tussocks of now iridescently golden grasses. It felt wonderful.

Not for the first time my mind wandered to the timelessness of such journeys, and how multiple generations have travelled similarly for reasons of work, food and security. Whilst our rationale for doing so was undoubtedly worthwhile, it was arguably less essential. But I like to think that the sight of Loch Lyon (our final destination) evoked similar feelings of relief that the hills had been successfully navigated, and (as the light was now rapidly fading) solace in the knowledge that we could safely descend. And descend we did. Grasslands springy with moss aided our gambol down to the lochside before the inevitable long trudge out.

We handed Rabbie over to the omnipresent Paul, faithfully waiting at the head of the road in the Archie van, and as he headed off on his bike, we hopped into the van and drove off to our rendezvous point for the night – a wild camping site halfway up Ben Lawers. I escaped the midges and folded myself into my car. There were plenty of recruits to take on the Challenge from here on in, and so I made my way home. By two in the morning I was safely tucked up in my warm, clean bed. The contrast between this and the previous 72 hours was so stark as to make it somewhat surreal.

Whilst I wouldn't say that taking part in the Archie Challenge has changed my life, it has opened my eyes to a whole subculture of hill running that I was previously ignorant of. The simplicity of running through beautiful surroundings and over varying terrain holds a great deal of appeal to me. It's no coincidence that a year after the Archie Challenge I completed my first mountain race, by taking part in the Lairig Ghru marathon. A few familiar faces on the day reminded me how special the Archie Challenge was and how proud I am to have taken part in it.

Waiting for the paddlers on the shore of Loch Etive at Taynuilt. Photo: Nicky Conway

DAY 15
13 June 2015
14 ARCHIES

113. Schiehallion

112. Carn Mairg

111. Carn Gorm

START

114. Meall Greigh

115. Meall Garbh
116. An Stuc
117. Ben Lawers

121. Meall Ghaordaidh

119. Meall Corranaich
118. Beinn Ghlas

122. Beinn Heasgarnich

120. Meall nan Tarmachan

123. Creag Mhor

124. Ben Challum

FINISH

GLEN LYON TO SCHIEHALLION

111. Carn Gorm (1029m), 112. Carn Mairg (1041m), 113. Schiehallion (1083m): Kirsty Maguire & Katherine Lawlor. 19km (1710m)

ROAD CYCLE

Schiehallion car park to Lawers village: Paul Fettes. 26km (440m)

LAWERS GROUP

114. Meall Greigh (1001m), 115. Meall Garbh (1118m), 116. An Stuc (1118m), 117. Ben Lawers (1214m), 118. Beinn Ghlas (1103m), 119. Meall Corranaich (1069m): Des Crowe & John Hepburn. 22km (2080m)

TARMACHAN

120. Meall nan Tarmachan (1044m): Andrew Murray & Joe Symonds. 4km (600m)

ROAD CYCLE

Cycle from Lawers car park to Glen Lochay: Paul Fettes. 14km (150m)

MEALL GHAORDAIDH

121. Meall Ghaordaidh (1039m): Kate Annan & Katy Boocock. 8km (880m)

ROAD CYCLE

Glen Lochay 'road' cycle link: Paul Fettes. 8km (260m)

GLEN LOCHAY TO STRATHFILLAN

122. Beinn Heasgarnich (1078m), 123. Creag Mhor (1047m), 124. Ben Challum (1025m): Joe Symonds & Andrew Murray. 23km (1810m).

*Distance in kilometres, (and ascent in metres – this is the cumulative ascent of the leg, even if there is a net descent and the finish is lower than the start). In some cases there was a walk (or run) in or out to the start or finish of a leg without carrying the baton.

Run meets walk: Glen Lyon to Schiehallion

By Katherine Lawlor – with Kirsty Maguire

I was pleased to meet up with Kirsty on the final weekend of the Archie Mountain Challenge. I had planned just to do the days in the north-west but having been back at work, and feverishly watching the tracker outlining Rabbie's route through the Highlands, I couldn't resist another chance to join in with the fun in some hills closer to home. Our route took us from Camusvrachan in Glen Lyon to Schiehallion (1083m), via a ridge of hills which included Carn Gorm (1029m) and Carn Mairg (1041m). This involved another absurdly early start after camping for a few hours' kip. The invigorating wake-up brew was spoiled a little by the swarming midges, but it did reduce the usual procrastination.

The run over the ridge was mainly in the mist, no snow drifts this time, and required some careful but satisfying micro-navigation. We approached Schiehallion by stealth from the south side, scrambling over boulders to the top and surprising some walkers on the summit. It was all we could do not to boast about our heroic and lengthy approach route to these hill walkers who had stuck to the conventional path. On our way down, two very energetic young men came sprinting uphill towards us. It turned out to be Joe Symonds and Andrew Murray, who were taking video for coverage of the Challenge on *The Adventure Show*. For this we decided we should probably do some proper running. With a great dose of fortune and absolutely no engineering, our run happened to coincide with the Schiehallion 'community' hill walk. We speeded up still further to the cheers of the Archie families, and it was great to see familiar smiling faces of friends and colleagues, spurring us on as we carried Rabbie down the hill. I am proud to say that several seconds of video of our ankles made it onto national television. Our incoherent ramblings to camera fortunately never made it past the first edit.

Rather less fortunately this was my last leg in the Archie Mountain Challenge, which for two short weeks in June provided a splendid adventure, an opportunity to meet mental and physical challenges, appreciate the wild and beautiful places in Scotland and work as part of a team to realise a fabulous idea. There was a tremendous sense of achievement and euphoria for all involved in completing the Challenge. This was later followed by a melancholy sense of loss and lack of purpose once it was all over. Reliving those weeks a little by writing this leaves me with a question: What is the next challenge to be?

Gary Tompsett
June 13, 2015

Wow! Is Rabbie going to meet the Schiehallion walkers this morning? That is mint!

 6

👍 Like   ➤ Share

Walkers on the summit of Schiehallion. Photos: Mark Tuddenham

Old Dogs on the Lawers Six

By Des Crowe – with John Hepburn

It was not the nicest of days for a run up some big hills but Paul and his crew had a plan, we had a start date, and nothing was going to stop us helping the Challenge along to its completion.

My old running pal John 'Heppy' Hepburn and I had the task to help Rabbie the ARCHIE rabbit over the six Archies of the Ben Lawers range. We were meeting Paul off his bike at the Ben Lawers Hotel at a given time, give or take an hour.

We sat in the van, drinking coffee, chatting and hoping the rain would go away. The rain went, and as Joe Symonds arrived in his car he brought news of Paul's impending arrival, and instructions on how to use his 'techie' watch, which would do everything except help us up the hill. Ha ha! As if two old dogs like us, with over 60 years of hill experience between us, would need such a thing! We did have a map and John, as back-up since it was such a poor day, had an app on his phone to help in the event of uncertainty. All sorted.

Paul came in beaming with joy after his bike ride, and Rabbie was hidden away in the top of my bag so he could be tracked by 'T'internet'. Off we went at a trot up the first hill, Meall Greigh (1001m). A quick check of the map and compass and then off to the second hill, Meall Garbh (1118m). We successfully navigated through the mist over An Stuc (1118m) and on to Ben Lawers (1214m). Now, you have to understand the mentality of runners when the excitement gets into you. This is when you start to follow a path and no matter what factual information is laid in front of you it will take something very big to happen before you alter the course. It was at this point that Heppy's phone began to ring... The call failed but we had come to a stop so we looked at the map and compass and finally at the app. Oops! We had descended the wrong way off Ben Lawers. Surely not! So, with the help of John's app, we retraced our route and this time, after removing our runners' heads, we took a correct bearing for Beinn Ghlas (1103m). All went well to our final hill Meall Corranaich (1069m) and after some photos of Rabbie we headed down to the bealach and the Ben Lawers car park, where we met the crew. Job done.

After handing over Rabbie to Andrew Murray and Joe, we chatted to Paul and the rest of the team about the run, only to find that because Rabbie had a tracker on his back they knew we were off route long before we did – in fact the phone call to John was to warn us of our mistake. They had been watching and ranting at us to change route, but luckily for us we are a lot slower these days, or the mistake could have meant a much bigger climb back up to the summit.

Quick Trip up the Tarmachan
By Joe Symonds – with Andrew Murray

Andrew Murray and I took the baton off Des and John at the Lawers car park, high on the road between Killin and Glen Lyon. At just two miles in distance, this must have been one of the shortest running legs of the Challenge. Flexibility was one thing that the Archies Challenge handled very well. Andrew and I were informed that we would be doing this leg about five minutes before the runners appeared off the slopes of Beinn Ghlas! The idea of this last-minute change of plan was to give us more of a rest before our evening shift, whilst Kate A and Katy B went up and down Meall Ghaordaidh. Our main challenge on Meall nan Tarmachan (1044m) was to make sure that we'd reached the true summit in the thick mist. In less than an hour we were back down at the car park, passing the baton on to Paul for the first of his two cycle legs up Glen Lochay.

Meall Ghaordaidh
By Kate Annan – with Katy Boocock

After 24 hours of washing Lycra and following the tracker from afar, I rejoined camp Archies Mountain Challenge in Glen Lochay. Cameron McNeish describes Meall Ghaordaidh and its surrounding mountains as 'undistinguished'. I feel that he just lacked the company of Katy B – her enthusiasm for the mountains, mountain marathons, cyclo-cross and knitting got us around the muddy manholes to the summit, and then back down again with constant chatter and smiles all round.

I feel privileged to have been involved in this venture at all. I went in with trepidation that I would hold up the relay, but felt that I was whole-heartedly welcomed by everyone and embraced as part of the team. For anyone else still suffering from AMC withdrawal, or those who regret not being able to take part, I would definitely be interested in doing it all again!

Kate Annan and Katy Boocock on Meall Ghaordaidh. Photo: Kate Annan

Unexpected Welcome in a Dark Place: Glen Lochay to Strathfillan

By Joe Symonds and Andrew Murray

Joe: When Andrew and I took the baton back from Paul at 8pm at the head of a massively potholed road in Glen Lochay, we knew that we would be in for a challenge. The climb up to the summit of Beinn Heasgarnich (1078m, magically translated from Gaelic as 'peak of the roaring waterfall of the horses') would be tough but straightforward. Thereafter, navigating over the grassy saddles and ridges to Creag Mhor (1047m) and Ben Challum (1025m) in fading light and thick mist would require concentration and vigilant compass watching. On the way up Heasgarnich we saw plenty of waterfalls but no horses, and were rewarded for our climbing efforts with a glorious run in the twilight along the summit ridge. We managed to get to our second Archie, Creag Mhor, in the dusk, but soon after we left the summit, just after 10:30pm, we were in full darkness. The terrain between Creag Mhor and Beinn Challum was surprisingly complex, with us having to drop down into the Allt Mhic Bhaidein and then over the saddle of Cam Chreag, then another drop to the Bealach Glas-Leathaid, before the final ascent of Ben Challum. Coming off Cam Creag we went a little too far west and found ourselves much lower into the Gleann a'Chlachain than we wanted. Once we'd re-found our bearings, our mistake forced us into a heavy slog back up the steep slopes of Ben Challum. After summitting our final Archie of the night, we descended in heavy rain to the end of our run at Kirkton Farm in Strathfillan, arriving just after 1am. Here, having expected to be pitching a tent for a damp night, we had the most unexpected welcome. Archie Mountain Challenge participant Giles Ruck, in his role as organiser of the Caledonian Challenge Ultra, which was finishing in the very same place that night, had managed to find us a warm and dry cottage! In five hours' time I would be up again for three more Archies with Graeme (five times more rested than I was before my last leg with him!).

Andrew: It's fair to say I was toiling trying to keep pace with Joe while he chatted away, explaining what the names of various Archies meant in Gaelic. I recognised Schiehallion as 'Fairy Hill of the Caledonians', and various names involving horses and long white tails, but think the 'mountain of the unicorn with a sore knee' might have been a hoax. Negotiating the last two Archies of the day in the dark led to various wrong turns, a couple of tumbles, and ensured that the soup that we had at the end tasted a good deal better than the 79p it cost from Tesco.

DAY 16
14 June 2015
6 ARCHIES

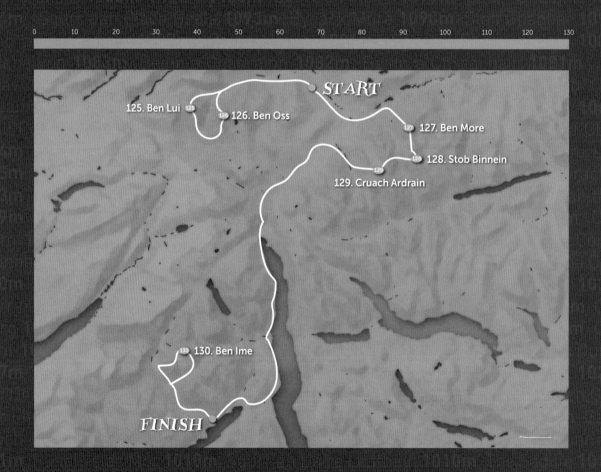

START

125. Ben Lui 126. 126. Ben Oss

127. 127. Ben More

128. 128. Stob Binnein

129. 129. Cruach Ardrain

130. 130. Ben Ime

FINISH

BEN LUI AND BEN OSS
125. Ben Lui (1130m), 126. Ben Oss (1029m): John Irving, Calum Grant & Grant Rodney. Cycle 18km (320m), run 9km (1060m)

CYCLE LINK
Katy Boocock. 8km (90m)

BEN MORE TO CRUACH ARDRAIN
127. Ben More (1174m), 128. Stob Binnein (1165m), 129. Cruach Ardrain (1046m): Graeme Gatherer & Joe Symonds. 16km (1860m)

SHORT RUN
Short (–50m) running leg in a car park on the side of the A82: Struan Gatherer (8) & Mairi Gatherer (6)

ROAD CYCLE LINK
Cycle to Rest and Be Thankful: Lynn Gatherer, John Hepburn & Des Crowe. 36km (650m)

BEN IME
130. Ben Ime (1011m): Grant Rodney, Calum Grant, Kate Annan, Kirsty Maguire, Giles Ruck, Katy Boocock, Joe Symonds, Paul Fettes & Maisy the dog. 8km (840m)

CYCLE LINK
Rest and Be Thankful to Ardgarten: Kirsty Maguire, Katy Boocock, Kate Annan & Paul Fettes. 8km (50m)

ATLANTIC TOE DIP (LOCH LONG)
Anna Fettes (9), Struan Gatherer (8), Mairi Gatherer (6) & Paul Fettes

FINISH 16.59
Duration 15 days 9 hours 6 minutes.

*Distance in kilometres, (and ascent in metres – this is the cumulative ascent of the leg, even if there is a net descent and the finish is lower than the start). In some cases there was a walk (or run) in or out to the start or finish of a leg without carrying the baton.

Ben Lui and Ben Oss

By John Irving – with Calum Grant & Grant Rodney

I'm just a girl who cain't say no

I'm in a terrible fix

I always say, 'Hey, come on, let's go'

Just when I oughta say nix

From the song 'I Cain't Say No', in Oklahoma!

Words by Oscar Hammerstein, sung by Ado Annie Carnes

The Archies relay accelerated south, homing in on a Sunday finish that had seemed highly unlikely. I watched the efforts of the rabbit carriers from my sofa, online, well out of the way. The weekend had been ruled out for participation as I was committed to a Spa session in Edinburgh, and Sunday lunch with old friends. Paul called. Were we interested in a final return to the fray?

So Katherine was meeting Kirsty at midnight on Friday on the Ben Lawers road, camping in the midges, running over Carn Mairg and Schiehallion, and then coming back to Dundee. I would then meet Calum Grant and Grant Rodney in the Real Food Café in Tyndrum. All of the camper vans had gone home, but we had been kindly invited by Giles Ruck to find some floor space in the farmhouse headquarters of the Caledonian Challenge. A 03:00 start would leave enough time to climb Ben Lui and Ben Oss in time to finish with Ben Ime that afternoon, and also, let me get to One Spa on time.

The recent extremes of weather had relented. Neither winter storms nor summer heat were on the cards, just hill fog and rain. Rolling west along Loch Earn-side, I reflected on the appeal of a snatched trip to the Southern Highlands. This was the landscape of my first teenage steps into the hills, from trudging along the West Highland Way under a monstrous rucksack, to day trips with my Dad to bag Munros in ones and twos. I had revelled in the recent days among superstar hills of Torridon and the Cairngorms, but a return to homely places fills another need.

I was most of the way through a chicken curry at the Real Food Café when my companions arrived, weary from the trails, lean and laconic like a pair of Montana cowboys. They shovelled away their fish suppers readily enough, and smiled at the right places in my tales of Cairngorm Zombiehood, and we all headed back to Cal Chal HQ. We found we were many drinks behind most of the party. One girl was channelling Carmen Miranda with an entire fruit bowl attached to her hat. We settled down out of the way on the floor of the front room. The door opened a few times and more people dossed down. Certainly some were Archie runners, but I began to lose track of things.

Alarm. I awoke into a very full dark room, head torches lighting pale slumbering faces. Quick cup of tea, and out into heavy rain. (Strathfillan was mentioned on BBC weather that evening as the wettest place in the UK!) One minute on our bikes along the track to Tyndrum, we passed the huge party marquee at the finish of the Caledonian Challenge. Floodlights lit up the sheets of rain, disco classics and excited commentary rattled over the PA, cagoule clad cheerleaders applauded home the teams of race-numbered dark figures. We cycled against the flow of people littering the forestry trails and single-track, all waymarked with regular tape. Turning into the woods was like stepping out of a smoky pub into clean air.

We could turn off the head torches as we pedalled up the empty glen in grey light, sweating in our waterproofs. The farmhouse at Cononish was properly quiet, no barking dogs as we slipped past. The deep streams flowing off the hill required care and momentum to cross; we ate up the miles without mechanical issues. Leaving the bikes, we kept the pace on the front foot as we strode up into the corrie, and into the mist. The ground was saturated around patches of granular snow, some slimy rocky scrambling focused the mind, and then we were on the summit of Ben Lui (1130m). It seemed too early to be one hill from home, and I wasn't sure whether to break out more than an apple for breakfast. We debated whether the northerly top 200m away might be higher, but the map was fairly clear. We trotted down the ridge, to the bogs on the col.

Ben Oss (1029m) throws a broad grassy ridge down to the col. The most exciting point of climbing this was when I found an abandoned selfie stick. I later impressed the children by demonstrating how you can use this to drop your iPhone into a mug of tea. The summit of Ben Oss was misty cold and wet, and we departed down the steep grass to the north, losing all of the height in a 15-minute trot, before wading the burn back to the bikes.

Back at the farmhouse, it was still only breakfast time, and the atmosphere was similar to what you might expect in a rented holiday cottage, the night after a group of friends have turned up well-supplied with whisky. Seven barely started boxes of tea bags covered the table. Breakfast was mostly biscuits. Our return triggered Katy Boocock to cycle into the rain, with Joe Symonds driving off in hot pursuit so that he could be in place to run the next leg with Graeme Gatherer. Peace descended. The end of the Archies relay seemed assured for this afternoon's schedule, and mellow contemplation was the order of the day. I slipped away from the group, and down the wet road to Edinburgh with Andrew Murray for company. Later, as I stretched out my legs in the rooftop Jacuzzi overlooking the Western Approach Road, my mind wandered, partly I have to admit to the enormous lunch waiting round the corner, but partly back to the hills, and to a group of like-minded people running in the clean sunshine of the Arrochar Alps, hauling a funny idea to a conclusion.

Penultimate lap: Ben More, Stob Binnein and Cruach Ardrain
By Graeme Gatherer – with Joe Symonds

This was my third helping of the Archie Challenge, and it proved to be just desserts! This was the second time that I had been paired up with Joe, who had set a searing pace in the blazing sun on our last outing together. Thankfully, this time his efforts the previous day slowed him to a more reasonable pace. Still, the long slog up Ben More (1174m) near Crianlarich was done hastily and I was glad of more typical Scottish drizzle to keep me cool. We enjoyed massive snowflakes on the top and remarked on the total contrast in weather to our previous outing. Compass bearings were the order of the day and we made fast progress over Stob Binnein (1165m) and then over to Cruach Ardrain (1046m), the penultimate Archie of the Challenge. It wasn't long before we were below the cloud again and descending the ridge down to Glen Falloch. Keeping things in the family, we handed Rabbie over to my kids, Struan and Mairi, who raced along the layby to hand Rabbie over to their Mum. Lynn, joined by Des Crowe and John Hepburn, made short work of the cycle southwards via Loch Lomond, Loch Long, Arrochar and on up to the Rest and be Thankful where Rabbie was handed over to make an ascent of the final Archie, Ben Ime.

The Last Archie: Paul, Calum, Joe, Giles, Katy and Kirsty on Ben Ime. Photo: Grant Rodney

Rest and Be Thankful: 'The Last Leg'

By Paul Fettes – with Grant Rodney, Kate Annan, Joe Symonds, Kirsty Maguire, Giles Ruck, Katy Boocock, Calum Grant, and Maisy the dog

It was a relief to watch the cyclists appear at the layby on the road up to the Rest and Be Thankful. It seemed ironic to think that the cycle down the A82 had struck me as more hazardous than most of the other stages of the Challenge. The team had successfully battled its way through blizzards, heatwaves, gale force winds, and torrential rain. It had scrambled along knife-edge ridges, navigated over remote cloud covered plateaus in the dark, and kayaked over storm-swept waters. It would therefore have been cruelly ironic if Lynn, John and Des had been taken out by some nutter effecting one of the high speed overtaking manoeuvres that is seen all too commonly on the ribbon of tarmac that winds its way along the west bank of Loch Lomond.

There was almost a party atmosphere as eight people and a dog set off up Ben Ime (1011m). It was a rather dreich and misty Sunday afternoon, but this did little to dampen our spirits. We made our way at a relaxed pace up a rather feeble path that headed north-east along the side of a stream towards the Bealach a'Mhaim. From there we headed north up a broad grassy ridge to the rocky summit. Although the torrential rain of the previous night had abated, there were still some darkly angry looking clouds around, and mist hung around the tops of the surrounding hills. But it was starting to clear, and we were treated to shards of sunlight as we approached the summit cairn. At the top we took our time to savour panoramic views, and I could finally reflect on a remarkable adventure, and the fact that a rather eccentric idea had been made a reality. There were handshakes and hugs, and smiles all around. Perfectly on cue Calum retrieved a bottle of Champagne and some plastic 'glasses' that he had somehow managed to hide in his small rucksack. So we toasted reaching the top of Archie number 130, our final summit. We took some group photos, and filmed Katie doing a one armed cartwheel. I wish alcohol had that effect on me.

Then it was time to head back down. This time we skirted round the eastern slopes of Beinn Luibhean, headed back over peat hags and steep grassy slopes, over a horse-tail of waterfall, and down to the car park at the Rest and Be Thankful, where we rested awhile, and were thankful. We were greeted by my wife Heidi, my daughter Anna, and my parents Peter and Mary, who had driven across Scotland to share the moment. Likewise, Gillian and Mark Tuddenham with their young son Euan had made the effort to be there, and they had gone to the trouble of erecting an Archie Mountain Challenge banner for us. As the skies cleared, and the sun warmed the air, I realised that we were fulfilling my rather hopeful vision of finishing on a sun-blessed weekend afternoon, with friends and family around to share the moment. It seemed a long way away from the dark days after my head injury. In many ways this whole journey had been an answer to prayer. God does indeed work in mysterious ways.

Another bottle of bubbly was shared around the many. After enough time to enjoy the moment, and take a few photos in front of the banner, four of us set off on bikes down to sea-level on the shores of Loch Long. Katy B, Kirsty and I cycled our own bikes, and Katie A joined us on a borrowed steed, which was slightly too large for her, as was the helmet. For once this small bundle of energy looked slightly ungainly on her newly adopted mode of transport. Perhaps one for the future, Katie! There was no rush, and we had the luxury of using the traffic-free military road for most of the way. This seemed a good idea until we were most of the way down it, and were faced with a sea of cow dung to cross! Thankfully this was cycleable at a slow pace, so we arrived at the shore of the loch no more fragrant than before. About twenty or so folk were there to witness Rabbie having his paws dipped in the Atlantic Ocean, under improbably blue skies at around 5 pm. Fifteen days and nine hours had passed since his first encounter with salty water in the North Sea, and in between he had been the sole creature to scale all 130 Scottish mountains over 1000m high, in what had very definitely been a bonkers and wonderful challenge.

Toe dip in the Atlantic Ocean: Paul in Loch Long at Arrochar. Photo: Peter Fettes

The Challenge? It was a piece of cake. Photo: Paul Fettes

We had a ball. Photo: The Courier

Outside the Arrochar Inn. Photo: Peter Fettes

Winding up

Aftermath by Paul Fettes

A warm reception at the Village Inn.

The Village Inn enjoys a splendid vantage point on the shore of Loch Long in Arrochar, overlooking the Arrochar Alps, of which Ben Ime is one. It is a fine establishment, and a great place to hold a little celebration after climbing a mountain, or two, and especially after 130! This place also held a special significance for me, as my Dad had worked as a GP here for many years, and was still well-kent and respected in the area. This rather impromptu and low key celebration was perfect for the moment. There was a relaxed buzz as we enjoyed food and drink, and each other's company. Then all too soon it was time to go home, and back to a normality, which at least initially, felt a little strange.

Soon there were reports of 'tracker withdrawal'. What could people do of an evening rather than feed their addiction to following a small dot on a map? I suppose it is inevitable that something containing so much in the way of excitement and camaraderie can leave people feeling a bit flat afterwards. But all good things must come to an end, and there was still sponsorship money to chase, a barbecue chez Fettes for those involved, and a Gala Dinner to organise.

We had a ball

Three months later, in September, we had the Gala Dinner in the Apex Hotel in Dundee. Tickets sold out quickly for this, which was a relief for the organising committee but left some people disappointed. I suppose that is a good problem to have, and the fact that the largest venue in Dundee was full to the gunnels was testament to the local popularity of the event. Or perhaps it was just a good excuse to party.

Conclusion

I would like to think that we achieved what we set out to do. In total we raised just over £33,000. The Challenge featured in the national press, and on The Adventure Show. This helped raise the profile of The ARCHIE Foundation in Tayside, and kick-started the appeal to help furbish a new paediatric theatre complex in Ninewells Hospital.

So far over £33,000 raised for the Archie Foundation!

Why go ARCHIE Bagging?

by Russell Duncan

WHY GO ARCHIE BAGGING?

What is Bagging?

Bagging is the name that's been given to the activity of collecting mountains. It's a bit unfortunate, really, because it suggests there is a kind of 'hunt and gather' aspect to the endeavour. You're never going to take an Archie home for the pot, but you may bag a brace or more on a single day.

What is an Archie?

An Archie is a Scottish mountain with a summit over 1000m above sea level – they are the biggest mountains in our islands and a trip to the top of each one is an experience worth collecting. When Sir Hugh Munro decided some 130 years ago to collate a register of all the mountains in Scotland that were above 3000 feet tall he did so not because he just liked the number 3000 but because he wanted a list of the highest mountains – not the prettiest or the most remote, the highest. It really strikes a chord, doesn't it? People have sung songs about climbing the highest peaks as a metaphor for doing whatever it takes, and Sir Hugh knew the effect the high mountains could have on the human spirit, so he compiled his list. We reckon if Sir Hugh had been alive today he would have come up with our list, but as it stands the 'Archies' is a brave new list of Scotland's highest mountains – the 130 that stretch more than a vertical kilometre into the sky with no higher top nearby that you don't have to descend at least 100m to reach – it's like the Munros but there are fewer of them, and they're all massive. Even the purists have got to love that.

Scottish Domination

Forget football. At least when it comes to mountains, Scotland dominates the rest of the UK. There are 130 separate mountains in Scotland over 1000m. There are only four more in the whole of the UK and they are all in Wales. with none in Northern Ireland, and none in the whole of England!

An achievable bucket list

The Archies are accessible, fewer in number than the Munros and more achievable. First, there are no island Archies. They are all in the Highlands, and none are in the far north. The most northerly is the great An Teallach, the most westerly is Ladhar Bheinn and the most easterly is Lochnagar – all fabulous iconic peaks. Look at a map of the Archies and you will see them congregated in clusters around the great landscapes of Scotland – the Cairngorms, Royal Deeside, Rannoch Moor, Glen Lyon, Glen Etive and Glen Coe, the Nevis Range, Knoydart, Kintail, Torridon and the Great Wilderness. Crikey – no-one on the planet should need to be asked twice to be whisked off to these locations, and how better to get to grips with them than climb to their highest points and survey the scene before you!

Second, there are only 130 Archies rather than 282 Munros. That's an awful lot easier to fit in to a busy life. Having said that, it is also a good halfway house if you want to go on and complete the Munros.

Third, while the Cuillin ridge on Skye is stunning and well worth a visit, the Inaccessible Pinnacle and the TD Gap are technically challenging and have been a stumbling block for many Munro baggers. Well, the good news is that none of the Archies are more than a decent scramble, making this an achievable bucket list for almost every hill walker who knows to carry a waterproof and how to read a map.

But why go Archie bagging?

It may not be a hunt but there is a real satisfaction and feeling of achievement associated with bagging a mountain and the Archies are the shortlist of the biggest, grandest, loftiest and most majestic mountains in the UK. If it's an achievement to bag one, then why not collect them all? In doing so you will get the opportunity to travel the length and breadth of mainland Scotland. You will experience true wilderness with all its natural beauty and native flora and fauna. You will definitely see the largest and most majestic of British mammals, the red deer, but if you are lucky you might also come across wild goats on An Teallach, golden eagles in the Cairngorms, and ptarmigan, mountain hare, red squirrels, black grouse and lots more in between.

The Archies list takes Munro's list and brings it into the modern age without taking anything away from it. It's not definitive for the great mountains of our islands – no list is. Many great mountains lie well short of 1000m in height – Goat Fell, The Cobbler, Stac Pollaidh and Suilven, to name just a few, but these aren't Munros either. There are a few notable Munros that don't make the list, such as Beinn Alligin, the Cuillin and Ben Lomond. These are all great hills and should certainly still be climbed, but they are simply not high enough to qualify. It is a definitive list of those mountains that stretch a kilometre towards the heavens, and that's surely a good place to start!

You can walk them, climb them, run them, ski them, or cycle them. You can't paddle up any, but you could paddle to the base of plenty. You could bag some in spring, the heat of summer or the icy splendour of winter; sometimes you could do all of this on the same day! For those who love to explore, challenge themselves and experience all that the nature of Britain has to give I suppose the real question is, 'Why not bag a few Archies?'

Extreme Challenge

A call to arms for those among you who are athletic or just plain nuts.

This book tells the story of a human powered relay over all 130 Archies, starting and finishing at sea level. If you are part of a hill-walking club, a mountain running club or an adventure racing team, then could you emulate us? Perhaps you could beat our time. If so, we would be delighted, especially if you raised money for the ARCHIE Foundation in the process. As you will read in the individual accounts of the challenge, it will be guaranteed to be memorable, for the most part will be seriously enjoyable and will almost always be thoroughly rewarding.

For the extreme adventure athletes among you, there is the scintillating prospect of a massive challenge which has not been done before. You could complete our entire challenge, but do it all yourself. If you were fit enough and quick enough, you might even be able to squeeze the whole trip into a normal period of annual leave, and still leave time for a massage and a decent pub meal at the end. Think about it. This will not make you rich, or famous (for that you would be better to enter Strictly Come Bake Me Out of Here, or perhaps sleep with an MP), but if you were to complete it then what an amazing achievement it would be, and what an incredible experience you would have in the process.

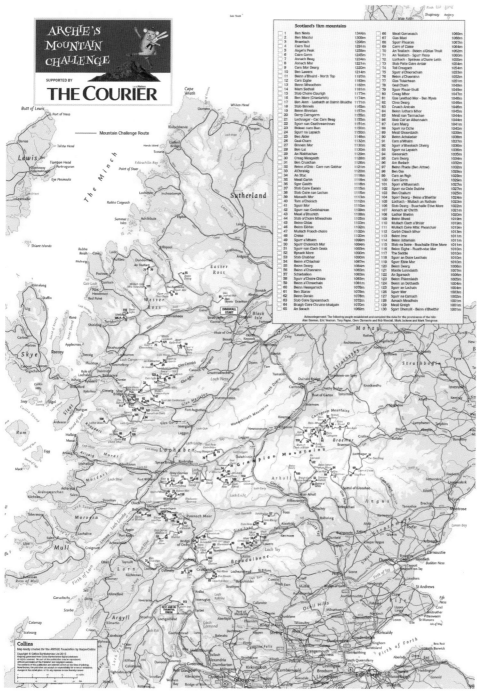

The Archies map as it appeared in The Dundee Courier. It shows the proposed route, one which we mostly followed although there were a few changes for logistic reasons.

Recommended reading

If this book has left you feeling that scaling Scotland's highest peaks will mean that you have conquered them and that that is all there is to it, then we have failed in our task. However if reading this book inspires you to spend more time in some of the most beautiful wilderness areas of our country, and having some sort of goal will motivate you to come back for more, then perhaps we will have achieved something.

For further reading by some people who appreciate spending time in the great outdoors, please consider reading some of the books on this list:

At the Loch of the Green Corrie by Andrew Greig – ISBN 9780857381361

Partly about fishing, partly about poetry, partly about Scotland's geography and rich history, partly biographical, but mostly just a beautifully crafted book by one of Scotland's finest authors, and one that knows and loves the mountains and the outdoors. This is simply one of the best books I have read.

Mountains of the Mind by Robert Macfarlane – ISBN 9781862076549

Although it culminates with an account of the death of Mallory on Everest in 1924, and the obsession that led him to that attempt, it is more an exploration into the lure of mountains, in all shapes and forms. It considers history, religion, understanding of geology and physical geography, as well as changes in culture and civilisation that have led to our current love of and respect for these wild places, and our obsession with reaching some of the highest peaks.

Running High by Hugh Symonds – ISBN 9780948403910

In the spring and summer of 1990, a very good hill runner called Hugh Symonds took some time off work as a teacher to run over and between the 277 Munros in 67 days. He sailed to Mull, and rowed to Skye. He then continued running to the Lake District and then on to Snowdonia, running over the 19 other separate 3000-foot summits there in another 16 days. Remarkably he then ran to the ferry, and went on to link the seven mountains in Ireland in another 10 days. Thus he ran over and between all the 3000-foot mountains of Britain and Ireland in 97 days! He was supported by his wife Pauline and three kids in a camper van. This account of Hugh's journey is full of appreciation of the beautiful places he was visiting, and is also peppered by accounts from his wife Pauline and each of his three children. What an amazing thing to experience when you are growing up.

Two of Hugh's children, Joe Symonds and Amy Manning, took part in the Archie Mountain Challenge. They both have links to Ninewells Hospital. Joe was a medical student in Dundee, and when the book was written was training as a paediatric neurologist in Glasgow. Amy is an obstetrician and gynaecologist, and husband Steve (who also participated in the Challenge) was an anaesthetist in Ninewells at the time of the Challenge.

Hell of a Journey: On Foot Through the Scottish Highlands in Winter
By Mike Cawthorne – ISBN 9781841830056

In the winter of 1997-98, Mike Cawthorne walked from Sandwood Bay (although I don't quite get why) to Glencoe, over most of or all of the 1000m Munros. He did this mostly alone. This is an account of another incredible journey and will be enjoyed by some for the sheer effort of his will in accomplishing this feat in the most inhospitable of conditions, although it makes bleak reading in places. His journey differed from ours in many ways, but the important one to point out is that he went over a different set of mountains.

The Living Mountain: A Celebration of the Cairngorm Mountains of Scotland
By Nan Shepherd – ISBN 9780857861832

I have not read this book yet, but here is what Amazon have to say about it: 'In this masterpiece of nature writing, Nan Shepherd describes her journeys into the Cairngorm mountains of Scotland. There she encounters a world that can be breathtakingly beautiful at times and shockingly harsh at others. Her intense, poetic prose explores and records the rocks, rivers, creatures and hidden aspects of this remarkable landscape.

Shepherd spent a lifetime in search of the "essential nature" of the Cairngorms; her quest led her to write this classic meditation on the magnificence of mountains, and on our imaginative relationship with the wild world around us. Composed during the Second World War, the manuscript of The Living Mountain lay untouched for more than thirty years before it was finally published.'

Feet in the Clouds: A Tale of Fell Running and Obsession
by Richard Askwith – ISBN 9781781310564

If you are intrigued why anyone in their right mind would run over hills for fun then you should read this book. Richard Askwith is a journalist with the Independent and an exceptional writer. This book won him the Best New Writer prize at the British Sports Publishing Awards and the Bill Rollinson Prize for Landscape and Tradition, as well as being shortlisted for the William Hill Sports Book of the Year Award and for the Boardman-Tasker Prize. Although he started as a London based novice, his enthusiasm for hill running is so infectious that by the time you have read this you might even want to try the sport for yourself!

Burn on the Hill: The Story of the first Compleat Munroist
by Elizabeth Allan – Limited edition
Reviewed by Peter Fettes

Collated from the diaries of Ronnie Burn, who was a sort of minister who lived in the south of England, and spent all his holidays taking the train up to the Highlands and walking, and walking... Like me he was a short-legged hunchback and a social misfit; his navigation was pathetic and he was not competent even with a railway timetable. His travels were from 1914 to 1927, and give a fascinating picture of how the glens were alive with all sorts of rural families, from whom he used to sponge accommodation and food – mostly gallons of milk. When I read it, it gave me a vividly different picture of the many empty glens I've traversed alone and in company. And it wasn't really so long ago when you think about it. World War One was partly to blame.

Mountaineering in Scotland by W.H. Murray – ISBN 9781898573234
Reviewed by Peter Fettes

For sheer love of the high places of Scotland this book takes some beating as it was written in an Italian P.O.W. Camp, in tiny writing on toilet paper I think, completely from memory, was discovered by the guards and destroyed, so he started again from scratch. He lived in Lochgoilhead, where I was one of the GPs, and died at 83. Usually sold as a single volume with Undiscovered Scotland.

Hamish's Mountain Walk by Hamish Brown – ISBN 9781905207336

The first continuous Munro round, and superb book, bursting with stories and nuggets of information. A total classic.

Elspeth's watershed blog:

This is not a book, but if you would like to read about Elspeth Luke's Watershed 680-mile run up the backbone of Scotland from Peel Fell in the Borders to Duncansby Head in the far North East then visit:

www.watershedscotland.blogspot.co.uk

Other big Scottish adventures...

www.ramsaysround.com

Charlie Ramsay completed his Ramsay Round (mentioned by Graeme Gatherer is his Easains account on Day 9) over 24 Munros in 23 hrs and 58 minutes. I was there by the dam on Loch Trieg as an eight year old in my parents' camper van. My Dad helped support Charlie, who also taught me how to swim.

www.gofar.org.uk

Contains details of many other mountain challenges, including the Broxap Round. In 1988 Jonathon Broxap went over 29 Munros in 24 hours, in the Kintail and Affric area. It also describes the Lakeland classic the Bob Graham Round, described in some detail in Feet in the Clouds.

The ARCHIE Foundation

by Kevin McCormick on behalf of the ARCHIE Foundation

In January 2014 The ARCHIE Foundation was launched in Tayside to support fundraising activities dedicated to 'Making the Difference for children in Tayside Children's Hospital'.

In November 2014 it launched a £2 million appeal towards creating a new, twin-operating-theatre, paediatric surgical suite alongside the existing children's Ward 29 and outpatients. This will replace the existing children's day case surgical Ward 30 with its single paediatric operating theatre, which is located some distance from the rest of the Children's Hospital. When complete the new surgical suite will enable many more of the children requiring surgical procedures at Ninewells to be cared for in dedicated paediatric facilities. It is hoped that this will be the first of many projects in a long term relationship between The ARCHIE Foundation and NHS Tayside.

2016 saw the first ever public art trail of its kind in Dundee when 70 wonderfully decorated sculptures of 'Oor Wullie' adorned the streets of the city throughout the summer in Oor Wullie's Bucket Trail, to celebrate the 80th anniversary of this lovable character and to raise vital funds for the Tayside Children's Hospital appeal. The bucket trail was a huge success with massive public engagement. Over 15,000 people came to view the statues in the last weekend alone.

The ARCHIE Foundation was first formed in Aberdeen in 2000 to raise money to 'make the difference' between an excellent new children's hospital planned by NHS Grampian and a world-class facility with many extras which would make the experience of children being in hospital as good as it can be for the children and their families.

The charity funded important structural changes to the new children's hospital, additional staff, research, specialist courses, many pieces of specialist equipment, emergency grants and much more. This enables The ARCHIE Foundation to 'make the difference' between the excellent clinical care delivered by the NHS and a child friendly environment which makes any time spent in hospital, long or short, a better experience for the child and their family.On 25th January 2014 the Royal Aberdeen Children's Hospital (RACH) was 10 years old and had had over one million visits from children and their families through its doors, leaving it in need of some TLC itself.

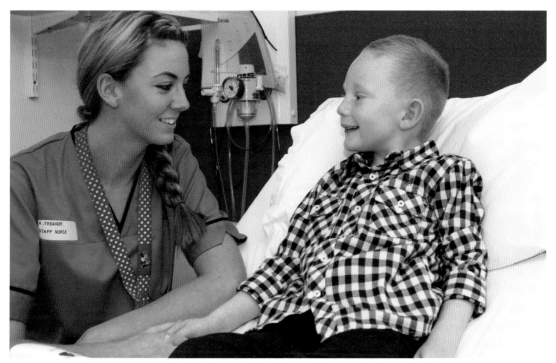

The Archie Foundation. Photo: ARCHIE Foundation

The ARCHIE Foundation launched a 10th anniversary fundraising appeal 'High 10 for ARCHIE' with the vision 'To make Royal Aberdeen Children's Hospital world-class for today and tomorrow's sick children. ' Following a period of successful fundraising, work has begun on the upgrades at RACH and will continue throughout 2016/17.

In March 2011 The ARCHIE Foundation launched an appeal in the I lighlands to raise £1 million to refurbish the existing children's ward in Raigmore Hospital, Inverness. This sum has been surpassed and £2 million has been raised, enabling a paediatric unit to be created, bringing all the paediatric in-patient services together in a whole new Highlands Children's Unit with its own dedicated entrance. The children moved into this wonderful new facility in May 2016 with staff, patients and families all delighted with their new surroundings.

The ARCHIE Foundation also supports many other child healthcare facilities across the north of Scotland, in smaller hospitals and community based projects. The charity has become a trusted brand in fundraising for child healthcare, always promoting its desire to 'Make the difference' for local sick children in every area in which it operates.

For more information visit: www.archiefoundation.org

WWW.ARCHIEFOUNDATION.ORG

JUMP

TRANSFORMING CHILDREN'S HEALTHCARE

THE ARCHIE FOUNDATION

MAKING THE DIFFERENCE

Specialist Independent Financial Planning advice for medical and dental professionals

Medical + Dental Financial Planning Services brings a wealth of experience in delivering impartial specialist advice, understanding client's needs and building relationship based on trust. We help you on your financial journey to formulate financial plans/strategies and work with you to implement the changes to develop, manage and protect your wealth.

- NHS & University scheme pensions
- Retirement Planning
- Investment Management
- Risk & Protection Planning
- Estate & Tax Planning
- Mortgages

www.medicaldentalfps.co.uk

9 Dudhope Terrace Dundee, DD3 6HG
info@medicaldentalfps.co.uk
01382 205938

MEDICAL+DENTAL
FINANCIAL PLANNING SERVICES
DEVELOP · MANAGE · PROTECT

Medical+Dental Financial Planning Services Limited
is authorised and regulated by the Financial Conduct Authority

Acknowledgements

Book

Compiled and edited by Paul Fettes.

Graphic Design by Gregor McNeish.

Additional editing by a former colleague, now retired, who rather typically declined to be acknowledged.

Additional proofreading and editing by John Irving, Andrew Dalton, Heidi Fettes, Peter Fettes, Keith Brunskill, Iain Belford, Hilary McNally, Miranda Fettes and Mary Fettes. Your time, patience and suggestions are much appreciated.

IT and administration Chris Kennedy.

All the costs of publishing the book have been covered with substantial sponsorship by Medical + Dental Financial Planning Services, and by a very generous donation by a member of the ARCHIE Foundation Tayside Fundraising committee.

The Challenge

Nick Leslie – Help with initial definition of the Archies.

Prominence data: Alan Dawson, Eric Yeaman, Tony Payne, Clem Clements, Rob Woodall, Mark Jackson and Mark Trengrove.

Gary Tompsett and Nick Leslie helped with initial route design.

Gillian Campbell – Overall planning, first weekend and digital map/route work.

Ben Ulyatt – Overall planning, communication and challenge registration.

Suzie Byer, Fiona Drimmie, Gillian Campbell and Jillian Walker – Organising the first weekend.

Mountain Leaders on Ben Wyvis walk: Andy Acton, Peter Derrick, Steve Byer and Brian Coghlan.

Coordinators – Nick Leslie, Kirsty Maguire, Russell Duncan, John Irving, Ben Ulyatt and Jason Hardy made sure people were assigned to each leg.

Route planners – Nick Leslie, Kirsty Maguire, John Irving, Gavin Miles, Matthew Bull, Matthew McCullagh, Gary Tompsett and Tim Gomersall – detailed route, timing estimation, hazards, handovers etc.

Kirsty Maguire – Individual stages spreadsheet.

Website - David Cunningham (ARCHIE) and Chris Kennedy.

Grant Rodney for his role in bringing ARCHIE to Tayside in the first place.

ARCHIE – David Cunningham general support and website, Emma White first weekend, fundraising/sales and general support, Hannah Clark fundraising/sales and general support, Kevin McCormick publicity/press, David Tipping Website and T-shirt artwork extraordinaire, Jillian Walker first weekend, Cassie Thompson fundraising.

Gala Dinner organising committee: Emma White and Hannah Clark from ARCHIE, Grant Rodney, Lezley Cassidy, Suzie Byer.

Camper van support vehicle – my Aunty Liz Fettes.

Food – Kath Bain large box of food.

Home baking – Fiona Bull, Kate Zealley and Karen Pearson.

First aid kits – Russell Duncan.

Alison Geddes – bagpipes on first weekend.

Accommodation – Russell Duncan, Jason Hardy, Gillian Campbell and Giles Ruck let us use accommodation they owned or had rented during the Challenge.

Mark Beaumont for supporting the Challenge concept, publicising it and doing his best to take part (though circumstances did not allow), and writing the Foreword.

Andrew Murray for supporting, publicising and taking part.

Andrew Murray and Joe Symonds for helping to film and record on the last weekend

Rabbie for getting over 130 mountains enduring snow, rain, hail, sunshine, gales and total submersion without falling apart.

My parents for their love and encouragement, and for engendering my lifelong love of the outdoors.

And finally Heidi Fettes for supporting her husband in almost every conceivable way through a nasty head injury, and throughout the Challenge.

SUPPORT

Medical + Dental FPS for providing significant corporate sponsorship for the challenge.

The Courier for supporting and publicising the challenge in a very significant way

John Clark Motor group – Combivan support vehicle.

HarperCollins mapwork – Ewan Ross and Kathryn Kelly.

The Storehouse of Foulis by Dingwall for hosting the start and providing free coffee and bacon sandwiches.

Marks & Spencer for providing wine for the quiz, water, and apple juice for the first weekend.

Go Outdoors for providing water bottles and electrolyte drink sachets.

Dundonnell Mountain Rescue for attending the Ben Wyvis walk (although I hasten to add they were not needed!).

Triple Echo Productions for filming for The Adventure Show. Richard Else and Margaret Wicks of Triple Echo productions for their time and attention, and for buying me lunch!

Mapyx for providing the Spot tracker and internet support to enable us to follow the progress of our amazing team.

The Village Inn, Arrochar for hosting a wee celebration at the finish and providing sandwiches for everyone.

Apex Hotel, Dundee for hosting the Gala Dinner at charity rate.

My Dad for paying for a bottle of wine for each table at the Gala Dinner (as a demonstration of gratitude, an ad hoc collection on the night roughly matched his donation. I suspect the free booze also made people more inclined to buy raffle tickets and to splash out in the auction, which was good news for fundraising).

The band 'Eat the Peach' for providing such great entertainment at the Gala Dinner,

Gary Robinson from Wave 102 for acting as MC and auctioneer for the evening.

Also everyone who helped in any other way. You know who you are…

PARTICIPANTS

The main challenge had 57 participants – listed in chronological order:

Paul Fettes (Anaesthetist), Ben Fettes (Paul's son), Barry McGuire (Anaesthetist), Rory McGuire (Barry's son), Chris Kennedy (IT maestro), Vicky Alexander (Paediatrician), Andrew Kilpatrick (GP), Craig Cumming (Anaesthetist), Ben Ulyatt (Anaesthetist), Simon Crawley (Anaesthetist), Claire Hardy (GP), Kirsty Duncan (Pharmacist), John Irving (Cardiologist), Jason Hardy (Anaesthetist), Russell Duncan (Emergency Physician), Nick Leslie (Scientist), Grant Rodney (Anaesthetist), Kathryn Lawlor (Paediatrician), Katy Boocock (Paediatric Physiotherapist and erstwhile Adventure Race Organiser), Peter Ferguson (retired, erstwhile Adventure Race Organiser), David Roberts (GP), Kirsty Maguire (Architect), Elspeth Luke (Musician), Matthew McCullagh (SQA Quality Manager), Gary Mooney (Psychologist), Andrew Forrester (GP), Colin Donald (Emergency Physician), Giles Ruck (Chief Executive of Foundation Scotland), Pete Ross (ENT surgeon), Matthew Bull (Policeman), David Henderson (Financial Planner), Richard and Fiona Maguire (retired), Jamie Smith (Fish Farming Executive), Neil Fettes (Farmer), Graeme Gatherer (GP), Phil Lacoux (Anaesthetist), Alan Carson (Psychiatrist), Tom MacEwan (Psychiatrist), Tom Fardon (Respiratory Physician), Steve Manning (Anaesthetist), Amy Manning (Obstetrician & Gynaecologist), Calum Grant (Anaesthetist), Mike Donald (Emergency Physician), Kate Annan (Emergency Physician), Joe Symonds (Paediatric Neurologist), Brian Stevenson (Dentist), Nicky Conway (Paediatrician), Andrew Dalton (Anaesthetist), Gary Tompsett (Adventure Race Organiser), Tim Gomersall (Medical Student), Gordon Wishart (Panel Beater), Katie Sims (Client Support Advisor), Des Crowe (Electrician), John Hepburn (Auxillary Nurse), Andrew Murray (GP and Sports Medic), Lynn Gatherer (Business Owner).

"My one enduring memory of the Challenge was meeting and interacting with so many positive and capable people. I cannot express how humbling it was to watch (on the tracker) team after team putting in such Herculean efforts again and again. Thank you to Paul and everyone else for the opportunity to join one of the most special events I have ever taken part in – never has the phrase 'standing on the shoulders of giants' seemed so apt." Matthew McCullagh

View from the Alder group towards Ben Nevis and surrounding summits. Photo: Graeme Gatherer